HOW I BECAME ME

HOW I BECAME ME

Danielle Clift

Copyright © 2012 by Danielle Clift.

Library of Congress Control Number: 2012910279
ISBN: Hardcover   978-1-4771-2626-4
            Softcover   978-1-4771-2625-7
            Ebook   978-1-4771-2627-1

All rights reserved. No part of this book may be reproduced or transmitted in any form or by any means, electronic or mechanical, including photocopying, recording, or by any information storage and retrieval system, without permission in writing from the copyright owner.

This book was printed in the United States of America.

To order additional copies of this book, contact:
Xlibris Corporation
1-888-795-4274
www.Xlibris.com
Orders@Xlibris.com

CHAPTER 1

"DANIELLE, COME INSIDE, YOU HAVE been out there for hours, my mother said for what seemed like the hundredth time." just five more minutes' please mom. As I sat on the curb looking at the ground between my feet, I watched a long line of ants march in a perfect line. I couldn't help but wonder where they were going. I caught myself wondering if all these little ants had daddies too. I had waited for what seemed like an eternity for my father to come and pick me up for his weekend visit. It was already past dinnertime and the sky was already dark, except for one street light that flickered across the street from my house. I sat there staring at every car that went by wondering and hoping if this one would be my dad. It never was. After five long hours of sitting on the curb with my suitcase, hunger and exhaustion got the best of me and I went inside. When I walked in the front door, my mother came, wrapped her arms around me, and told me how sorry she was for what my father had done again. I was so young then, I did not understand why my dad never wanted to see me. After dinner, I went upstairs, to my room changed my clothes and crawled into bed. As I laid there wondering what it would really be like having a weekend away with just my dad, my sister and me, my door suddenly burst open, my sister was saying. "When are you going to get it?' he is never going to come visit us you are just wasting your time sitting out there on the curb waiting for nothing. I did not want to believe her words, because I felt in my heart that my dad really did love me. And that something bad most of happened for him not to show up again for our weekend visit. Right before I dozed off to sleep, I pulled my curtains open so I could see the street. Just in case he was really late, I wanted to be able to see his headlights if he pulled in the driveway. The next morning I woke up to the sound of my mother's voice call, Wake up Danielle, its time to get ready for school, I hated that time of day, I dreaded every moment that had anything to do with school. I remember every morning watching the kids hang out on the playground as I stood in the corner of the cement building alone, thinking that everyone hated me, and hoping that no one would notice me.

Once I got to school, I would walk into the girl's bathroom and I would hide in one of the stalls. I stayed there until the bell rang, and then waited for the silence that told me that all the kids and teachers were already inside the classrooms I somehow felt more Comfortable sitting alone in a dirty bathroom stall than I did most public places. I always hated being around a lot of people, restaurants, and birthday parties' shopping malls, anywhere that had crowds. Especially the school cafeteria, I never ate, no matter how hungry I was. I was convinced that the other kids were snickering and laughing at me.

Once the silence came that told me everyone was in class, I would cautiously sneak out of the bathroom, keeping an eye out for proctors and other personnel that might ask me why I was not in class. I would walk towards the back of the grass field and jump the small cement wall that led into the golf course. I always walked along the inside of the golf course to make sure that the truancy police would not see me. There had been too many times to count when the cops had found me, called my mom, and returned me to school. They recognized me instantly, knew me by name. I was tired of dealing with that. Once I was on the golf course I was able to relax. I would walk home, knowing that my mom was already at work and my sister was at school. It was so comforting to know that the rest of the day was going to be just my dog and me. It was my usual routine, to go to school, sneak out, and walk home. But one day I thought to myself, what's the point of walking all the way there, just to turn around and come back. So on one particular day, I got up and got dressed and said goodbye to my mom as usual. Then I walked downstairs, opened, and closed the front door so she would think I left. Then I sneaked quietly back up stairs to my room and crawled under my bed. I soon realized that my mom did not leave for work as early as I thought she did. I continued to lay there and listened to my mom getting ready for work. She was listening to 'crazy" by patsy cline on her record player. She really loved patsy. I smelled the smoke from her cigarettes and heard her get in the shower. My legs were starting to get tingly from being still too long and I had to go to the bathroom really bad. Two hours later, she finally left for work. It had been more than an hour since I peed my pants. I didn't care, the way I saw it, hiding under my bed laying in my own urine with cramped legs was a lot better than having to go to school. Finally, I was able to pull myself out from under the bed. I changed my clothes that were wet and cold from the urine. I grabbed a dirty towel and threw it over the wet spot under the bed. I went downstairs and made myself a quesadilla; that is practically what I lived on. I was too young to cook and since my mom worked so much she was never home. Most of my days were spent inside the house playing with our dog. She was an Australian dingo and Shepard mix. She was bright orange with a white face and huge chocolate colored eyes. She looked like a deer so we named her doe and she was my best friend, my only friend.

 My mother was always my hero, even though she never knew it. She always seemed so glamorous to me. I remember watching her get dressed for work, she wore her hair in a bun high on top of her head. She wore dark blue eye shadow and bright red lipstick. Her uniform was a very short skirt with ruffled panties and a tight laced bodice that pushed her boobs together so tight that it must have been hard to breathe. She was so beautiful to me. My mom's "wonderful" "glamorous" job was working the night shift at a popular restaurant as a cocktail waitress. I always loved going to the restaurant. It was a huge place with fake snow on top of the roof. On the inside, the floors were covered with sawdust and peanut shells. When you walked in the front door there was this huge grizzly bear that had been hunted and stuffed standing up on its hind legs. I was so fascinated with this bear, with its ferocious teeth bared and its front paws outstretched; I would just stand there and stare at it every chance I got. His glass eyes seemed to look right through me. It was beautiful to look at but it made me sad. I knew that, at one time he had a family of his own out in the forest somewhere, and that they had searched and searched for him, missing him.

My mom worked steadily, never missing a day, serving drinks to men who made catcalls and grabbed ass whenever they got the chance. Men who were sloppy drunk making comments to the beautiful waitress who worked so hard her arms felt like jello when she got home, and the corns on her feet left daily blood stains on her shoes and stockings. The hot burn in her left shoulder never went away no matter how much I rubbed it for her. She was a single parent trying to raise two young girls on her own without the help of any other family members, including our dad. She had told me years later that she was grateful that she had made friends with the cooks at the restaurant so that she was able to grab whatever food was left at the end of her shift so she could bring it home to my sister and me. If there was nothing left in the house to eat, I knew there would always be some cheesy bread and baked potatoes. I didn't understand my mother's sacrifice and struggle, I only knew that she was my hero and when I grew up, I wanted to be just like her.

Me and my sister were home alone all the time, babysitters were expensive. One night it was really late and my mom wasn't home yet. We waited and waited but she didn't come home that night. The next morning she came home and walked in the front door with a huge cast on her leg. She had fallen down at work and ripped some tendons in her knee and part of her kneecap was cracked. She said that she was going to sue them, but that she didn't have the money to do it right away and that it ouwld take along time. I didn't really understand what all of this meant but I did know that my mom no longer had a job. I thought it was cool because she home so much more but, it kind of sucked too because I had been spending the whole six hours of school days laying under the bed. The urine was so strong smelling that it was hard to breathe.

Two weeks after my mom's fall, she told us we had to pack our things. We were going to move in with our grandma. My mom was on disability and we could no longer afford to live in our tiny apartment. I was terrified, grandma? I did not even know her. The drive to grandma's house only took thirty minutes but it seemed like an eternity. I sat silent in the back seat as we flew down the freeway in our little blue Volkswagen bug. The windows were down and the sunroof was open feeling the hot summer wind on our faces. I'm not sure how we did it but, we had managed to get our most important belongings and our clothes to fit inside the tiny car. My sister and I sat in the back with Doe panting and drooling in between us. The only sound I heard the whole way besides the loud hot wind was the sound of my mother sobbing in the front seat. Somehow, I knew my life was about to change.

Chapter 2

WHEN WE PULLED INTO THE driveway there was a woman standing on the front porch with a cigarette hanging out of her mouth. My mother was the first one to speak. She said in an unsteady voice, "Girls, this is your grandmother." I remember thinking while I was looking at her that she must have been beautiful at one time. She was small and thin with bright red hair and piercing blue eyes. When she told us to come and give her a hug, I was hesitant. She seemed to have a problem standing and her voice was harsh and raspy from smoking for almost 50 years. My mom rushed us upstairs to show us our room. It had light blue carpet and blue and white striped wallpaper that was faded with a yellow tint from years of smoking. The curtains, old and dusty, were also blue. The room was empty except for one bed and an old wood nightstand under the window that had little tea cups and figurines on it. Instantly, I wanted to go back home. My sister and I sat on the bed and cried, we had only been there for a few minutes and my mom and my grandma were already fighting. I heard my mom saying, "She's staying, she is family and I don't want the girls to hurt any more than they already are!" We realized they were talking about Doe.

When I heard my grandma say she would not allow the dog to stay, I ran downstairs and outside to the car where Doe was panting and anxious to get out of the car. I grabbed her leash and walked down the driveway. I did not know where I was going, but I knew I would not let anyone take my dog away.

    I walked for a long time, not having any idea where I was going. I stopped and sat in the shade of a big tree in someone else's yard. I cried for a long time. Such loud sobs escaped my mouth that I was surprised no one inside the house heard me. It was starting to get dark. I got up, started walking again, and was trying not to be scared. I knew Doe would keep me safe. After a few hours I admitted to myself I was lost. I started to cry again . I walked up to a house and turned on the long green hose that was lying across the front yard. I let Doe drink her fill and then drank some myself. I did not realize how thirsty we both were. Someone from inside turned the porch light on and opened the front door. I told them I was just giving my dog a drink of water. When I tried to walk away they asked where my parents were. I tried not to cry, but the lump in my throat was too much for me. I broke down and told them that I was lost. I did not know my grand mother's address but I told them her name. The old man knew who she was. He offered to walk me home and I accepted. I wondered why he did not offer to drive me, but I figured it was probably because of the big orange dog growling low in her throat behind me.

    The walk home only took about 10 minutes. I felt dumb for being lost when the big blue house that was going to be my new home was only a short distance away. I thanked the man and started for the door when he insisted on speaking to my parents. He kept saying the word "parents" and it was irritating me. I corrected him and said "my mom." As soon as I opened the door I saw my mom's eyes were swollen and red from crying. She hugged me so tight it was hard to breathe, then she let me go and told me to go into my room while she talked to the old man. I told her I was not going anywhere with out Doe. She gave me a slight nod of her head that told me it was ok to take the dog upstairs, so I did. I crawled into the big bed with my sister and the dog and tied the leash tightly around my wrist, just in case someone tried to take her during the night.

We woke up the next morning to the sound of dishes clanking around in the kitchen. "Are you going to go down stairs?" my sister asked "Yeah, I guess so, lets go together." I replied. We left Doe in the room even though she was pacing back and fourth by the door trying to tell me that she needed to go outside. Once we got into the kitchen we realized it was our grandmother in there and not our mom. "Where's Mom?" we asked, "She went out to look for a job." Grandma said. She put some food on two plates and told us to sit at the table and eat. I think it was supposed to be oatmeal but I wasn't sure. Grandma told us to wash our dishes when we were finished. Once she left the room I grabbed my bowl and ran upstairs to our room and closed the door. Doe hungrily ate every last bit of the slop in the bowl. Thanks Grandma, I silently laughed to myself. I wouldn't want my dog to go hungry. Two days went by and I seemed to spend most of my days playing with some old dolls. I had found a box of old stuff in the closet. There was some pictures of people I did not know, a few stuffed animals, a pair of old ice skates and a lot of Barbie stuff. I figured this box belonged to my aunt Gwen Even though she had this amazing long blonde curly hair, we still had a striking resemblance to each other. I never got to see her much though. She was really smart and was always traveling to far away schools on the other side of the world. I used to wonder what it would be like to go somewhere different. I doubted I would ever be able to go anywhere else in the world except for the state I was born in.

Two months went by. One afternoon I was sitting down stairs in the den waiting for my mom to return. She was at the doctors today getting her brace off her leg. When she walked in the room I ran to her and hugged her tight. Now she could go looking for a job and we could get out of here soon.

The next morning I woke to strong gusts of wind coming in

through the windows causing the thin, dusty, blue curtains to flap wildly. The sun was completely blocked, only dark gray clouds for as far as I could see. I knew that rain was coming soon.

I was relieved when it was finally bedtime. Glad to have one more day over and done with. And glad that my mom would be coming home from job hunting soon.Right before I fell asleep I jumped to the rumbling sound of thunder, and Doe whining beside me. I felt the whole house shake, it felt like the whole house was going to split in half. Then the rain started. It started raining so hard that it sounded like thousands of little rock pouring down on top of the house. Huge, pounding drops coming down in a torrent. You couldn't even see across the street it was raining so hard! The lightning flashes outside the bedroom window were constant, giving me a glimpse of the damage the gusting wind had done to the trees and shrubs out in the back yard. My sister and I sat there in the bed with Doe and we all three huddled together and tried as best we could to comfort each other. An hour into the storm, the arguing started. We heard my mother and my grandmother yelling and screaming at each other. We tried to lay down under the covers and pretend this was not happening. Then we heard loud crashing sounds. We both jumped up out of bed and ran downstairs to see what was happening. We stopped on the middle of the stairs and started pleading for them to stop. They were both on the floor. My mom seemed to be holding grandma down on the floor, shouting at her to calm down.

At that moment there was such a loud crack of thunder we thought the house had been hit. Everything was instantly dark. I felt Doe run down past us on the stairs. She was frightened from the storm. We heard my mom yelling for us to go back upstairs. We felt our way back up to our room and crawled underneath an old wicker laundry basket. We sat there in the darkness for what seemed like a very long time and held each other. A few minutes later the power came back on so we went back downstairs to see what was going on. We saw our grandmother with a rope in her hands walking toward

Doe who was cowering in the corner of the living room behind the grand piano. I heard my grandmother threaten "I'll hang that damn dog from the tree in the back yard!" My mom was trying to keep her away from Doe telling her that she should just go to bed. Mom glanced at my sister and I and told us to go pack our things, we were leaving. A few minutes later we had our few belongings stuffed into our suitcases. We walked down stairs and our mom led us out the front door towards the car. Once we got outside we realized we did not have anything on but our pajamas and our tennis shoes. The wind was blowing so hard our faces were stinging and the cold rain made us shiver. The car had a hard time starting due to the cold. Once the car was running and the heater was on my mom slowly pulled out of the driveway trying to see, with the windshield wipers smearing rain all over the window. Once again we were all packed in the car, headed some place new. We drove around for a while until my mom finally pulled up in the back of a small motel. She got out and told us to lock the doors and that she would be right back. I wondered why she parked all the way in the back and not up front by the lobby where everything was lit up. It seemed as though she was hiding something. Once she came back to the car she told us to leave Doe here and that she would come back for her in a few minutes. The inside of the motel smelled like old wet clothes and stale cigarettes. The dirty yellow wall paper was peeling off the walls in every corner of the room. We turned the heater on and a big cloud of dust came out of the vents and made it hard to breathe. Our suitcases were wet but we managed to find some dry clothes and socks to sleep in. Once we were settled my mom went back down to the car to get Doe. The four of all squeezed up together in the same little bed. The last thing I remember that night before I fell asleep was thinking how comforting my mom's small warm hands felt on my back. "Everything is going to be ok girls" was the last thing I heard. When we woke up in the morning my mom was on the phone. I heard her saying " I have no other choice, you have to take them. I will drop them off in the morning." The day dragged on but I enjoyed the four of us being there together. We ordered pizza and watched movies. Doe was pacing and whining by the front door, telling us in her own words that she had to go to the bathroom. I offered to take her outside for a walk but my mom told me that we could not risk her being seen by anyone because dogs were not allowed here. At about 7:00 p.m. my mom went downstairs to get us something to eat from the vending machines. When she came back her arms were full of chips, crackers, granola bars, and bottled water. We sat on the bed and started eating our dinner when we looked over towards the door and saw Doe go to the bathroom on the floor. It was a disgusting mess. I cleaned it up without complaining. When we were getting ready for bed my mom said that she was going to take Doe outside for a few minutes so we would not have a another accident on the floor. Once my mom came back she sat us on the bed and told us that we were going to go stay with our dad for a little while. Just until she got a job and got a new place for us to live. She made it sound like he was excited about having us. And I couldn't wait to see him. Right before we fell asleep there was a knock on the door, my mom told us to take the dog into the bathroom. When she opened the door we heard a man yelling at her in every strong accent, "No dogs allowed, you have to get out now!" My mother was pleading with the man but he refused to let us stay. We slowly came out of the bathroom and we saw the panic and fear on my mother's face. We did not have anymore money for another motel. Once again, she told us to get dressed and to pack our things. I was tired and wanted to go to bed. In the car, she told us to lay back and get as comfortable as we could and close our eyes and that we would have a bed waiting for us when we woke up. I started counting the street lights I saw through the back window. I lost count, then I drifted off to sleep on the backseat of the Volkswagon, between my sister and my dog.

Chapter 3

WE WOKE UP AT THE first sign of daylight shinning in through the back window. We were still inside the car. All the windows were fogged up from our warn breath hitting the freezing windows. I looked towards the front seat and saw my mom leaning against the steering wheel crying I climbed up front and crawled onto her lap and hugged her. I didn't think I needed to ask her what was wrong. We just sat and cried together.

I asked her where we were and she said we were at our dad's house but that he wasn't home yet. A few minutes later, my sister woke up. She was upset that we slept in the car all night and was complaining that she had to go to the bathroom. Let's get out of the car girls, there's a park right across the street and we can go use the bathroom there. We all four got out of the car and stretched our legs. Doe went to the bathroom as soon as her paws touched the grass. Me, my mom and sister walked over to the public restrooms and went to the bathroom.. We decide that since we could see our dad's apartment complex from across the street. That we would just sit and wait for him to return. By 1200 in the afternoon we finally saw an old green Chevy truck pull in front of the building and a tall dark skinned man hopped out and went into apartment #7. that's him girls, I heard my mother say. As we walked across the street I was thinking to myself, What if he doesn't want me . We knocked on his door and within seconds he opened it. he gave both my sister and I a huge hug and slowly slurred the words, I've missed you two so much. My mom asked him to come outothe car with him to help with or bags. We listened by the front step. And all we could hear was our mom crying, her words were not understandable. When she came back up the house she pulled us close and hugged us really tight for a long time. Only for a little while, ok girls my mother was saying. Be good and listen to your dad. As soon as I can I will come back for you. Then she let us go and walked towards the car. As she drove away, I cried. I cried for her sadness not for mine. I knew that this had to be a lot harder on her then it was on us. By mom, give doe kisses for me. We love you…….and then she was gone.. As we went into the tiny apartment we were shocked at how empty it was. It had only one tiny bedroom and a small kitchen with ugly dark brown counter tops and a dark green and yellow linoleum floor. The light brown carpet was thin and scratchy and covered with stains. The only furniture he had was a tiny old couch with the part of the material coming off on one corner, and an end table that had an old metal ashtray that was so full it had cigarette buts over flowing falling on the table. There was a small tv sitting on a top of two short stacks of playboy magazines pushed together as a makeshift table. He showed us his room and told us that we could sleep in his bed and that he would sleep on the couch. We set our small bags down in the corner next to the bed. He asked us if we were and hungry and we nodded our heads. He walked intot he kitchen and struck a match to light the small stove. He heated up the tortillas and spread mayonnaise and spam inside of them. It tasted good to us, the last time we ate was when we had the granola bars and chips from the vending machine the night before.. while we ate my dad grabbed a beer from the fridge and walked over to the old couch and turned the tv on. I stood in the kitchen and stared at him. He was a very tall man with long thick dark hair that was pulled into a pony tail at the back of his neck. His skin was a lot darker than my sister nad me and his eyes were so dark they looked black. He had on the same necklace that I always remembered him wearing. It was a thin black rope with a real dried scorpion encased in glass at the end of it.

    When we finished our spam burrito we both went intot he living room and sat on the floor next to the couch. I didn't know what to say to him, I was scared and nervous and I was irritated at myself for feeling like that. I tried to reassure myself by thinking, he is so happy that were here. He loves us and has missed us all these years. Hes my dad.and all daddies love their kids right? As much as I tried to resuure myself, the anxiety inside me would not go away. The next morning my dad came into the room and told us that he was going to work and that we had to stay here alone until he got back. " don't go outside" was the last thing he said to us before he walked out the door. Hours and hours went by and he was still not home. We got bored and started looking at the stack of magazines under the tv. After we laughed and giggled at all the pictures of naked people inhis playboy collection we decide to make somethingto eat. All there was in the fridge besides beer was half a bottle of mustard, a jar of mayonnaise and some tortillas. We found the spam in the cupboard above the stove along with a big box of matches. I grabbed the box of matches and asked my sister if we should light the stove. She said it was too dangerous. I decided to do it anyways. I slowly struck the match on the scratchy brown strip on the side of the box. When the match lit I dropped it into the burner and the fire came on. I was kind of proud of myself. After we ate our lunch we waited some more. When dinner time came I lit the stove again.. soon after dinner we heard a lot of loud boisterous laughing outside the front door. When the door opened my dad stumbled in with 3 of his friends. He made an attempt to introduce us but they were all slurring so much it was hard to understand them. as. The three men sprawled them selves out on the floor my dad looked at us and told us to got bed.

That's when my sister told him that I had lit the stove . My dad looked at me and motioned for me to come over there to him. He asked me if I was lighting matches in the house nad I slowly nodded my head. He told me to come stand in fron of him and pull my pants down. The panic inside me made me freeze. When I just stood there he yelled in a loud strained voice " i said pull your pants down, and your underwear too" as I started to cry and slowly pulled my pants and my underwear down. He then told me to bend over. He stood up from the couch and pulled his belt from around his waist. The first lash was so painful that I couldent breathe. Then there was a nother and another. He was holding the belt in the middle so that his big silver belt buckle was what was making contact with my skin.as I pulled my clothes back on I felt the warm wetness of blood running down the back of my legs. I went to the room and crawled inbed and cried, I cried for my mom and for how much Imissed her soft comforting voice and her small warm hands rubbing my back. Assuringme that everything was going to be ok. The next morning we woke to the sounds of my dads voice. "I have to got o work again. You know the rules. I will be back later. The day dragged my. We were bored and sad and getting sick of spam and tortillas. After dinner my sister and I decide to take a bath. When I took my clothes off and climbed into the tub next to her she started crying. She was crying because she saw the purple square bruises all over me from the night before by the lashings of daddys belt. We sat and cried and held eachother until the water got cold. That night when he came home he had his friends with him again. They were so loud that it was impossible to sleep. When I smelled something strange I got up and walked into the living room. One of dads friends was smoking something, that's where the smell was coming from. I stood in the doorway for a moment and watched as they passed around an old album cover with white stuff on it . I was wonder why they were all sniffing it up their nose.

When he saw me he told me it was cold medicine and that I needed to go back to bed. As I lay there trying to fall asleep I was wondering how much longer until mom came to get us. I missed her terribly. The next day after dad left for work my sister and I realized that there were no more food left in the house. By two oclock we had searched all the cupboards in the kitchen. All we found was one can of condenced split pea soup and some mayonnaise left in the jar. We grabbed the soup and stabbed the top of the can with a butter knife until there was a hole big enough for a spoon to fit in. after the soup was gone we grabbed the mayonnaise and started eating spoonfuls right out of the jar.. dad came home early that day and saw us eating the mayonnaise and started screaming at us for eating all of his food. He was slurring and stumbling and I was scared. We instinctively hovered by the front door. He was outraged. He grabbed the mayonnaise jar from the kitchen floor and threw it at us as hard as he could. Since he was so wasted his aim was off and it hit the living room window and shattered it. he stood hovering above us in the corner and slowly spit out the words, go pack your things, he was taking us back to our mom. As scared as we were we managed to slip past him to the room. Were were out waiting by the door with in minutes. He walked us around to the back of the complex towards the old green chevy truck that we saw him get out of the day we came. He threw our stuff in the back and told us to get in. inside the truck were empty beer bottles and trash everywhere.. I did not recognize any of the streets we were on but I was not about to say anything to him or ask him any questions. After about twenty mintues he pulled into an alley and parked behind an old building. He grabbed our small suitcases and walked us up the the back entrance of what appeared to be some kind of paint or carpet store. He set our stuff down next to a huge green dumpster that was over flowing with trash. He then told us " go inside, your mom is waiting for you" and he hopped back into the truck and left. My sister and I grabbed our suitcases and went inside the store. We walked around and looked everywhere but we did not see our mom. The store kind of made me sad because I saw people walking around shopping for things for their home, new windows, wall paper, curtains. I imagined that they all had pretty houses with huge rooms and lots of windows.. A man with a nice suit and a shiny yellow name tag approached us and asked if he could help us. " we are looking for our mom," the man looked at us for a moment then told us to follow him. He led us to the back of the store and pointed up to the top of a ladder. There she was, when she looked down at us it was almost as though she didn't recognize us right away. We had not hardly bathed or combed our hair, and our clothes had not been washed. She came down from the ladder and threw her arms around us. That was such a happy moment for me. I knew I was safe again. When she led us out front to where her car was parked I eagerly looked inside and asked her " mom, wheres doe?" she looked at me and said with sad eyes, she is staying with a friend for a little while, just until we get our own place. When we climber inside the car it was hard to get inside. The seats had been laid down and there were pillows and blankets and food wrappers and a small battery operated alarm clock on the dashboard, that's when I realized she had been living in it for the past few days. I wouldent care if I had to live in it with her, I thought to my self. As long as we are together I knew I would be happy.

    From there she drove us to one of her friends house, her name was diane and she had a small little gray dog named trooper that I liked instantly. diane was tall with really poofy hair and eyebrows that almost conncted together. (It's funny, the little details. you remember from when you were young) she seemed really nice and she was going to let us stay with her for a while. After about two months my mom came home from work one day and told us the best news in the world. She had saved enough money so we could move into our own little condo on the other side of town.. we were so excited! She told us we had to wait 10 more days before we could move in. I was already packed before it was time for bed. I kind of liked staying with diane and Trooper, even though I often saw her sniffing that same white stuff up her nose like our dad did all the time.. the day finally arrived, we loaded up our few belongings and drove to our new home. The condo seemed so amazing to me and my sister. It had 2 bedrooms and a kitchen it was a small house at the end of an alley. We did not have anyfurniture but I didn't care, it was home.

Chapter 4

I DON'T REMEMBER A LOT about living in this house. I don't remember going to school or doing anything really, but I do remember one of my mom's friends bringing doe back to us. I was so happy. We had not seen her for about 5 months. And I had missed her every day I also remember my mom was working a lot. My mom had a live in boyfriend named mark. There was also a friend of marks who lived in the trailer that was parked in the driveway. He was always looking at porn magazines and he always gave me the creeps. I remember one night when my mom was at work mark and his friend called me into the living room and told me to take a puff of the joint they were smoking. I was scared of smoking it but they held it up to my mouth and told me to suck on it. After a couple of puffs, I started to cry because I felt weird. Once they realized I was high, they took my pajamas off and grabbed me by my ankles and held me upside down. I was scared and crying, they started to spin me around upside down, and I was crying for them to stop. They were laughing at me, finally they put me back on the floor and gave me my pajamas back and told me to go to bed. I decided not to tell my mom because I did not want mark and my mom to fight anymore. They used to fight all the time. Mark was an alcoholic and he would get so drunk that he often didn't know what he was doing. He would drink and come after my sister and I. We would run and hide. I was not scared. Doe always kept us safe. Mark hated her. One time when Mark was drunk he started to come after me. Iran and quickly hid under an old table that was in the backyard. Doe was standing In front of me. As he started to come toward me, she started growling and tried to bite him. She was my most favorite thing in the whole world. A couple of days after that I came home from school and I could not find my beloved dog. After hours of crying and searching, I heard some faint cries coming from the garage. When I opened the door I could not believe my eyes. There was a large table with a bag of trash on top of it. the trash was opened exposing all the old food and table scraps from the last few days. Doe's hind legs were about a foot away from the trash. Her front legs were tied together and tied up to the top part of the rafters on the ceiling. She was whining from the pain. She was being tortured. Mark came in behind me and told me that she got in the trash and that we was teaching her a lesson. I was helpless mark closed the door and told me she had to stay like that for 3 days. I hated him and I wished I could tie him up like that. That night my mom came home and untied her. I was so happy that she was ok. One night they were fighting while I was in bed and I heard a lot of loud screaming and things breaking. I hesitantly crawled out of bed and opened the bedroom door. What I saw in the hallway is a vision I will never forget. Mark was on top of my mom holding her down with a knife at her throat telling her " I could kill you right now" my mom looked over at me and told me it was going to be ok and that I needed to go back to bed . I don't think I went back to bed. I remember feeling protective of my mom. I was trying to figure out a way to get our mom and runaway. The next evening I remember standing out in the driveway watching Mark attempt to work on his truck when I saw the police come down the driveway. My mom came outside and told me to go inside. The police took him away and we never saw him again. I learned later that he had some warrants out for his arrest. I suppose my mom called the police on him and turned him in. after that we had to move again. Probably for our own protection. She had been working at the paint store for a while now so we had enough money to move into a little condominium in the city of Azusa Ca. we had a two bedroom 1 bathroom condo that had stairs in it and it even had a dishwasher. We had lived there for a few weeks when my mom told us the news that our dad was going to pick us up and visit with us for the weekend. It had been almost 2 years since I had seen him. I was so excited. I ran up stairs, packed my bag, and waited. My sister did not want to go. She was a little bit older so I guess she understood more than I did. My dad actually showed up this time. We climbed into his truck and went driving to some house that he told us was his. We parked around the corner from this house and snuck in through the back door. We were not allowed to unpack our things or answer the door or phone and we could not eat any of the food. It was weird. I didn't know at the time that our dads girlfriends parents were out of town and that he broke into their home. I kind of remember thinking wow! He must really want o see us if he is going through all this. We went to sleep hungry on the floor in the living room. He said he didn't want us to mess up the beds. The following morning he said that he was taking us to Santa's village. We were so excited. Its like a theme park, with small rides and cotton candy and clowns and real reindeer that you were allowed to pet. We pulled up in the parking lot and got out of the truck. We only took about 5 steps and my sister fell down and hurt her knee. I remember her crying, and I saw the blood running down her leg. There was some loose gravel stuck in her skin. Our dad pulled a red bandana out of his pocket, spit on her knee and rubbed his saliva all over the cut and then he wrapped it up with his bandana. We walked into the amusement park and went straight over to the reindeer. I loved them. They were so soft, gentle, and huge. Once we finally got bored with that we asked if we could go on some rides. He said no, we asked if we could go eat, he said no then we asked if we could go see santa and he said no. and that it was time for us to go. I think about it now and I realize he probably didn't have any money. Once we got back to the truck our dad pulled a bottle of scotch or whiskey out from under the drivers seat and took a long drink. We drove onto the freeway not sure where we were headed. Once he started going fast my side passenger flew open. I think he forgot to close it. as I started screaming my sister grabbed onto me and pulled me closer to her. My dad reached over and closed the door. I still remember being terrified that I was going to fall out of the moving truck on the freeway. We continued to drive and he continued to drink. I guess he was so wasted he could hardly drive. Soon after that I heard the sirens from a police car. They were behind us telling my dad to pull over. He reluctantly pulled to the side of the highway The police approached the car and helped him get out. They asked my dad if there was someone he could call to come pick us up. He started crying and resisting the police. He was sobbing and tears and snot were all over his face. The police were fed up so they threw him down on the ground and sat on top of him and handcuffed him. They threw him in the car .We sat in the truck motionless as we watched the police haul our dad away to jail. What a great weekend huh, I do not remember how old I was, but somewhere around seven or maybe 8.That was the last time I ever saw my dad.

CHAPTER 5

AS I GO THROUGH ALL the things I have written so far, I find myself thinking. Don't I have any good memories? I'm sure I do.,I guess I just can't remember them. Or maybe the bad stay in your head more than the good do. I don't know. As all of you who read this have visions of me and my life in your head I want to reassure you that I'm ok and that the things that have happened in my life have made me the person hat I 'am today. Anyway I'm not really sure where I 'am going with that, all I know is that I'm writing exactly what comes to mind. With hope that I can connect with some troubled youths out there who feel or have felt like they are all alone in this big huge world with no one to understand them. But trust me, you are not alone. Ok now where was i. oh yeah, they just hauled my dad away to jail because he was driving drunk with us kids in the car. So after my dad's girlfriend came to the police station and picked us up she drove us back to our mom's house. I don't remember her reaction to what had happened, I can only assume that I was too distraught so I spent the night in my room… a couple of years went by with nothing really major happening. I still continues to skip school all the time and I fought with my sister violently. I'm not sure if the way my sister and I fought was normal or not. There was almost always blood and biting and hair pulling. Hard to imagine two people growing up in the same house could be so different. When I think of it now it really makes me sad that I never had a real relationship with my sister. ... there was too much damage done to our relationship at such a young age. I guess we both just built up walls..I will just continue to keep my fingers crossed.

When I turned 11 years old I started smoking cigarettes. Its kind of funny because i remember the exact day that I started. I was swimming in the pool at the condominium complex and I jumped up and went to my friends and said " lest go smoke some cigarettes" and that was it. I probably didn't inhale for about 6 months but what did I know. I thought I was cool. I remember coming home and my mom would ask me if I had been smoking, I always said no of course, but she knew. It wasn't much longer after that I started smoking pot. I was in heaven. Everything was funny and all I did was laugh. There were no bad or sad thoughts that entered my mind. I wished I could have stayed high all the time... Soon after I started smoking marijuana, I started staying out really late. I was supposed to be home when the streetlights came on but that did not last long. When I sit here and write about this I feel like im there, on the corner of my street. Smelling the chlorine from the community pool and how I would always look out behind the condos and see all the green openness of the golf course. I would stay out really late,even by myself sometimes and I would just hang out on the golf course. Shortly after that I started running away. Staying out late soon turned into coming home later and later and then I would start to stay gone for a day or two. And a day or two soon turned into weeks. The year I was twelve years old was the year that changed my life. By the time I was twelve all the local police knew me by name. I was constantly being brought back by the truancy police during the day, and the local police at night. I found that I was roaming farther and farther away from home. The police were always asking me if someone was touching me, I found out later that they had investigated my mom and her boyfriend. They suspected that some wrongdoing was happening. Why are you running away Danielle? You can tell us. My only response was that I wanted to be with my friends. I see now how lame it sounds. One day while I was at home, but skipping school with a friend of mine I saw my friend pull out some cocaine. I knew exactly what it was from seeing my dad snort it up his nose all the time. "its only cold medicine" that's what he would tell me whenever her saw me watching him. So, me and my friends were sitting there and they started cutting up lines. "Hey Danielle, you want some? I remember him asking. I could not say yes fast enough. I remember having to say it in a casual way, as if I had done it all the time or something. Drugs were cool right. I was so excited to be doing the same thing my dad was. Maybe he would like me if he knew I did the same things he did. I think I was hoping that I might run into him somewhere in this huge world of drugs.

Chapter 6

EVERYONE I HUNG OUT WITH was older than me, by a lot,. I looked older though, because I went through puberty so fast that I had these huge DD size boobs on my chest. as soon as I turned 12... I always lied when I was asked my age. I was already into meth and pot and alcohol. I just did what ever was available. I started to get arrested at night (and In the day) instead of just being brought home. I got arrested for under the influence and possession of marijuana. That charge was what got me put on probation. And once I was put on probation every time I got involved with the police, it was a violation. I had to serve 6 months in juvenile hall when I was 12 for a grand theft auto charge. I went out with some of my friends one night. They picked me up in a big van that was painted army camoflauge. We were all sitting in the back of the van snorting lines drinking and smoking pot. I liked the way I felt,. I was not interested in alcohol when I was high on speed. The three other people with me were drinking heavily. We drove a few hours away to this quiet little community. It had white picket fences and mailboxes with flowers and crap on them. Lots of people left their garages open. That's why my friends chose this particular place.

We were driving all over the neighborhood stealing what ever was interesting to us. That included a lot of chamrange. By the time it was time to go back I was the only one who was not drunk. So they kinda talked me into driving. I was scared to death. I actually made it all the way to our city. And once I stopped at a red light I noticed that there was a cop car right behind us. So we got pulled over and that's when I found out that the van was stolen. Do you think anyone admitted that they stole it so that I would not get in trouble for it…nope. Anyway, I have so many stories like this I could go on forever. After I was released from juvenile hall I went back to live with my mom. I think I ran away again before the week was up. She called the police again and reported that I had runaway, which was a violation of my probation so I knew that the police were looking for me. I wanted to look different so that the cops would not recognize me so I shaved me head and left a little duck tail in the back. If it wasnt for my boobs I looked just like a boy. I liked being a boy. I rode a skateboard all over the city and wore big loose shirts. I only did this for a few weeks then igot arrested again. I remember I was sitting out at this park behind my condominium complex. I was high on speed.(This was turning into an everyday thing) sitting with a friend on a bench. It was late at night. I remember seeing a police car slowly turning towards the park. My friend was telling me to just act casual, I started to panic because I did not want to go back to juvy, when I saw the cop car make a u turn I leapt over the brick wall onto the golf course and ran as fast as I could for what seemed like forever. When I assumed they were not following me anymore I climbed the biggest tree I could find and tried to relax and cath my breath. After a fw minutes I saw some flash lights and heard the ferocious sound of dogs barking. I froze up in the tree. Well of course the dogs led the cops right to the tree and they had their guns drawn on me yelling at me to come down. They soon realized I was just a kid. I went back to juvy and stayed there for a about a month . this time the courts said that I was now a ward of the court. Which mean that they kinda owned me. I was scheduled to be placed in a suitable home for troubled girls.. its strange,I cant seem to remember the first one I got sent o. I do remember running away from there too. And then I ran away again and again and again..

Chapter 7

I REMEMBER BEING SENT TO a place that the courts called a soda bed. It was a temporary foster home. It was not a very far drive from where I lived, maybe an hour. It was in Los Angeles. I remember the house was painted a brick red color. The woman who was in charge was an old heavy set black woman who didn't give me a warm fuzzy. She seemed cold and angry. After a few hours there I realized I was the only white person there. not that I cared they were all black, but it made me feel like a freaking out cast. Once they showed me the room where I was going to be sleeping, I stayed in there. I was too uncomfortable to come out of the room and eat dinner with the rest of the girls. I just said I was not hungry. I was actually starving. I remember just staying in the bed I was assigned to.. The girl that I was rooming with was older than me, im not sure how much maybe she was 15 or 16. She was very heavy for a girl her age and showers were not one of her priorities.. at night time when I was lying in bed I could hear the sounds of her masturbating. Even thinking about it now,20 something years later and I still remember the disgusting way it made me feel. And the stench of unclean vagina permeated the room. I couldn't wait to get out of this place. I had been deciding where I would go and what I would do when I ran away. After being there for only a few days a new girl came. Her name was star. She was a white girl, with red hair, blue eyes and a large gap between her two front teeth. We instantly had a friendship. She was older than me, I think she was sixteen at the time and I vaguely remember her talking about how she had a baby back home who was living with her mom. It was Stars second day there and we decided we were going to runaway later that night. We hung out all day and just acted "normal". Once it got dark outside we both went up stairs to one of the rooms. She wanted to do my make up for me, I remember she had a dark blue eyeliner and she made me look like I had cat eyes. I thought I looked so fabulous. So anyway since our make up was done we decided to pack what few things we needed. We grabbed a pillow case and put our make up, some cigarettes a lighter and a change of clothes in it. Then we got a rope from the backyard and tied it to the pillow case and lowered it down out the back window.(it was a two story house) to the ground. Once we were ready we went down stairs and out the back door and told one of the girls sitting at the kitchen table that we were going outside to smoke. Once we were outside we grabbed our pillow case and started walking. Where are we going to go ? I asked. She replied and said that she knew some people in Hollywood who would help us get to her house in Oregon somehow. So we walked and walked and walked, finally after 5 or 6 hours of walking the city lights started to come alive. We are in Hollywood now she said. I remember feeling excited .The streets were busy with all kinds of people. People with piercings all over, people with Mohawks, prostitutes, homeless people, weirdo's, any type of person you could imagine. As the night went on we continued to walk around until she recognized an old building. It was old and rundown with boards on the windows and stuff like that. There was an old drunk homeless man sitting on the ground in front of the building. Star walked up to this homeless man and said hey Red,whats up? I was shocked she knew him. He had a little black dog tied to a makeshift rope. Aaww I remember how cute he was. I went and sat on the ground next to the dog. After Star was done chatting with the man we got up and headed inside the building. Before we entered the broken door the homeless man turned and asked me to come over to him. I walked over to him and he asked me if I could do him a favor and keep his little black dog for him. He said that he had no food for the dog and that the god seemed happy with me. Sure I said, I would love to. So I took the rope and he kissed the dog goodbye and thanked me. I always did have a thing for animals. So we walk into this building and knocked on a door, some guy with long black hair answered the door. Star and him hugged and chatted for a while and he said it was cool if we spent the night there and that he would give us some money and drive us to the train station in the morning. I remember thinking how good looking he was, anyway so we all had to sleep in his bed. I think I remember Star calling him Rock, that must have been his nickname or something. So Rock is laying in the middle of the bed and Star and I each on the side. Sometime in the middle of the night I remember waking up to the feel of his hand coming up my inner thigh i looked at him and told him not to touch me, he said for me not to worry about it because he was fixed and that I would not get pregnant. I attempted to push him off of me but I was so young and small, I was no match. He put his hand over my mouth so I would not scream and he climbed on top of me. I slid my arm away from him and reached over to the other side of the bed until I felt Star. I started to punch her to wake her up. She sat up in bed and said what the fuck is happening. Rock got off me and asked Star What the fuck is wrong with her? I remember shaking so bad that I could hardly talk. Star knew I was a virgin, it was something we had talked about on our long long walk. Star said to Him, shes too young Rock, take me instead. Before I even had a chance to get out of the bed Rock was mounting her. I grabbed the rope tied to the dog and carried him to the front door of the building. A few minutes later Star came out. I knew she was mad at me because I just fucked up our plans. I guess Rock was so pissed that he said he was not going to help us anymore. Know that I think about it im pretty sure he never had any intention too. By this time it was already late into the night, maybe around 2:30 ish. Star said that we needed to find a truck stop.. She said that we could probably hitch a ride with a trucker who was headed up towards Oregon. We walked and walked before we finally came across a truck stop. Danielle, I remember Star saying to me, if anyone asks im 19 and your 18 ok…. Ok I said back. After talking to a couple of truckers with no luck, we were starting to get discouraged and were wondering where we were going to sleep that night. Once we scoped out the area we decided we could sleep in the park down the street, maybe in the bathroom or something. As we were walking away from the truck stop someone called to us, hey,he said . you two girls need a ride somewhere? Yeah,said star. We are headed up towards Oregon, well I just happen to be going that way he said. Finally, I thought to myself,.not only was I cold and hungry and tired. I was kind of excited,. I felt like we were going on an adventure As we climbed into the truck, I remember it was warm and I was relieved because it was freezing outside. We hadn't been in the truck very long before the sun came up. You girls hungry ? we were very hungry and tired. He got off the freeway and we left the dog in the truck and walked into a MC Donalds. We sat and ate some breakfast and I saved a little bit for my new companion waiting in the truck. Before we got back on the road, Star and I had to go to the bathroom. After we went to the bathroom we walked back to the table grabbed our sodas and headed for the truck. As I stepped up into the truck I remember thinking how unusual my soda tasted, better drink it all he said, it will probably be a while before we stop again.

Chapter 8

I SUDDENLY WAKE UP WITH something extremely heavy on my back, what the fuck is happening I thought to myself. I could hardly breathe. It was him, the trucker. He was on my back with his knee pushing all his weight on my so I could not move. Everything looked blurry and I felt like I was spinning. I started to scream and cry. He grabbed me under my chin and pulled my head back as far as he could. . I heard the sound of duct tape, I quickly realized that I could not move hardly at all. I had been hog-tied. My ankles were taped together and my hands were tied together at the wrists. Then he pulled my ankles back and tied them to my wrists. I was on my stomach. Everything was starting to come into focus now. I looked over in the right corner of the truck bed and saw Star. She was hog tied too, but she had duct tape over her mouth and all around her head to cover her eyes. I remember seeing the little black dog lying next to her in the corner. I saw the tears on her cheeks running down from under the tape. I knew as soon as he pulled my head back that he was going to tape me up like that too. It was hard for me to move, not just because of him on my back taping me up but because I felt like I had no control of my muscles. I had to have been drugged. As I lay there unable to move, I start to beg him not to do this. I will do whatever you want, I said. Please please don't hurt us. Next he put a large strip of duct tape over my mouth and circled the duct tape all around my head and my eyes. Everything went dark. I remember laying there like I was lifeless For what seemed like hours. He was listening to country music on the radio up front; he was actually singing along and whistling. My hands, arms legs and feet were past the falling asleep stage. They were finally numb. I don't know how much time went by but it seemed like hours before I felt the truck stop. I had been trying to calm star down, I remember hearing her having a hard time breathing and I was panicking thinking she was going to suffocate. Next I heard the radio turn off and I heard movement up front. I felt him moving around and then I heard the sound of clothes ripping and moans and cries from star. It was making me crazy that I couldent see what was going on. Then I feel him next to me. He grabs the part of the tape where my ankles and wrists are tied together and he turns me over and proceeds to cut my jeans and shirt off me. He cut where he needed to and ripped off the rest. After my jeans and shirt were off then my bra and panties came off to. I remember him kind of laughing and saying things under his breath like ohhh yeah baby. Next he opened my legs apart and thrust his fingers into me. He started laughing again and grabbed my face and started to punch me in the face repeatedly, he then put his hands around my neck and started to choke me. Ok. I thought, this is how I am going to die. Dear god, please tell my mom that im so sorry for the way I treated her and that she is a good mom and that I don't want her to be sad.

    I could not hold my head up anymore, I remember giving up and going limp. His hands came off from around my neck and his fingers were thrust back inside me. Yeah, fuck yeah, I heard him say. You little virgin cunt, im going to fuck you so hard. I felt him cutting the tape that connected my feet to my hands. He pulled my legs out from behind me and pinned them down on my face with one hand while the other hand undid his big belt buckle. I remember tasting the blood going down my throat and the warm wetness running from my nose. I was more worried about how difficult it was becoming to breathe then I was about the noise of his pants coming down. I was also worried about star; I had not heard a sound from her. She is probably dead I thought… oh god please no please no. I'm dreaming right. Wake up I told myself. Wake up. Once his pants were down, he pulled me towards him and thrust himself into me with the power of a freight train. I couldn't scream from the pain because of the tape. He continued to thrust himself into me over and over again, after a few minutes he stopped and groaned and pulled himself out of me. Don't worry he said, I'm not done fucking you yet…..

Then I remember listening to him shuffle around, he even said a couple of things to the dog. He climbed back in the front of the truck, started the engine and drove off… I was suffocating and I had to check to see if star was alive. Since my hands and ankles were not tied behind me anymore, I was able to feel where the dog was. From all the wetness on my face from the blood, snot and tears, I was able to get the tape halfway off my mouth by pushing out with my tongue and I was able to breathe again. I inhaled deeply. Then I remember spitting the blood from my mouth onto my wrists and allowing the dog to lick it off with hopes that the wetness would loosen the tape. It was working and I was finally was able to free my hands. There was a curtain that was pulled closed so that no one could see in the cab of the truck. I remember moving very slow so he would not notice any movement. As soon as my hands were free, I pulled the tape up over my eyes. I could not pull it all the way off because it went all around my head and all my hair was in it. I moved over to star and whispered into her ear that I was free and I was going to untie her. First, I pulled the tape off her mouth so she could breathe better. Then I undid her hands by biting and ripping the tape. I hugged her and actually smiled. It's ok, it's going to be ok.

When I look back, I see that she was in total shock. She had a blank stare. We had to have a plan. He is going to kill us Star, we have to fight or at least try. I do not want to die without trying my hardest to stay alive. I untied star and myself and we sat there in the corner without saying a word for a long time. There is nothing back here we could use for a weapon, I said. Star, are you listening to me? We have to use our hands and feet. Next time he comes back here, we both have to attack him with all the strength we have. It is our only chance. All she could do was shake her head yes.

We felt the truck get onto a different road. It was not smooth like the freeway anymore, it was bumpy. I told her to get ready and I said no matter what, don't stop fighting. As I slowly moved back over to the other side of the cab, I saw how much blood there was. It was everywhere. I had been lying in the blood that came from my vagina and it painted me red, making me look like I was bleeding to death. I remember telling star, I'm fine, it's ok. I'm fine I'm fine. We crawled into the corners and waited for him to come back there. This was our only chance at staying alive. The truck pulled over and came to a stop and I heard him ask if we were ready to fuck. As soon as he opened the curtain, I went crazy, like an animal or something. I remember kicking him as hard as I could, trying to get his face or his crotch. I think I closed my eyes and just fought with all my strength. Stop it or she is fucking dead do you hear me. I'm going to kill her right fucking now if you don't stop. I figured he had a gun or a knife but when I opened my eyes, I saw that he had his thigh on stars neck holding her down. He had this type of huge nail, as if it was from a railroad or something, it was thick like a piece of sidewalk chalk. He had it pushing into her temple with one hand, and with the other hand, he had a hammer. I will drill this fucking nail into her head right now if you don't stop. How come she wasn't fighting, I didn't understand. I stopped fighting and promised him I would calm down.. He grabbed my ankles, pulled me toward him, lifted his leg up, and slammed his foot down on my neck. He pressed his big cowboy boot into my throat, stepped on me, and held it there. I remember struggling to get it off me, but there was no way. He was way too strong. He stepped on my throat with his boot until I blacked out. When I woke up I was retied, but with my hands and ankles tied together in front of me. I assumed it was for easier access for him. I lay there sobbing for hours. The tears and snot once again worked in my favor by helping to loosen the tape. I kept nudging the dog for him to lick me more. I felt like he was trying to help me get the tape off. I was only able to pull the tape off my mouth,, at least I could breathe again. After another couple hours went by we felt the truck come to a stop again. It was the same routine as far as him whistling and telling us to get ready for the fuck of our life. He came back this time but went to star first. I heard her muffled screams; I remember hearing him beat her. I still have the sound of his fist hitting her stuck in my head. The truck was moving around, maybe someone would see and come knock on the door and ask if everything was all right. Dear god, please let someone come. I heard him groan again and once he pulled himself out of her he threw her body up against the side of the cab. I was quiet trying to decide what he was doing now. You knew what you were in for, when you got that tape off your mouth. Didn't you.. you think your smarter than me. Huh? Is that what you think? I remember shaking my head no. next thing I know I felt him grab my hair and pull me up and turn me so that I was on my side and not my back. He lifted my leg up and forced something cold and hard into my vagina, since the tape was off my mouth I could not control the scream that I let out. I will fuck you with this hammer until you die if you try anything, do you hear me. Yes, I managed to say. Leaving the hammer handle inside me he grabbed my face and opened my mouth with his fingers. Once my mouth was open, he shoved himself into my mouth. I vividly remember not only the smell but also the taste of feces in my mouth. It hurt my heart to know what he had done to Star. It made me gag and vomit. He didn't care though, he called me a dirty fucking pig and told me I deserved to have shit in my mouth for trying to fight him. I could not breathe through my nose at all so I had no choice but to swallow down the feces and the throw up that was in my mouth, he continued to brutally thrust himself in and out of my mouth. I thought about biting it, but I still had the hammer in my vagina. Once he was done. He pushed me down and told me" at least your good for something" Then I just laid there motionless.. I think it was two whole days that went by, and within those two days there had to be at least six or seven times we were raped. I remember laying there next to star. We were able to whisper to each other because, once again the wet fluids on our faces was allowing the tape to easily come off our mouth. She kept telling me. It hurts, it hurts it hurts. I cant stand the hurt anymore. I know, I said, everything's going to be ok. We just kept whispering that to eachother.(I remember thinking She was older, she was supposed to be the one comforting me). I think he managed to go through a regular workday with us tied in the back Of the truck. I remember being able to see a glimpse of light through the tape. When that light was gone I assumed it was night time. I was right. After driving around for hours and hours, he pulled over again. He grabbed star first and dragged her out of the truck. I wasn't sure where he took her, I thought for sure he probably carried her off into the bushes to kill her and dispose of her body. A couple minutes later, he came and got me; he dragged me out of the truck and carried me to the back. He unlatched the two solid metal doors and told me to get in. I remember it smelled like sawdust, or wood. It was cold and echoed, that is how I knew it was empty. He climbed inside the back of the truck and retied us with our feet and ankles out behind us again. More than a day had passed, I could tell from the daylight that came in through some type of vent towards the top of the truck. Once the light was gone I knew it was nighttime. I remember thinking if I could somehow stick my finger through the vent that maybe someone would see. But I didn't have any fight left in me. He won I told myself, im going to die back here. Star and I huddled as close together as we could to try to stay warm. Our faces were close to each other's, the warmth of her breath on my cheeks was not only warm and comforting, it was reassurance that she was still alive. I hope my breath on her face did the same for her. As I lay there watching the light slowly come up and shine through the vent, I noticed (with what little I could see under the tape) that there was a spider on the vent. I laid there and put my entire focus on that spider. I remember watching it crawl in and out while it spun its web. He had a way out. As the tears began to fall again I eagerly licked them off my cheeks. They were warm, wet, and wonderful on my tongue. Star, how do you think we are going to die? Maybe we will pass out first and then we can stop suffering. Maybe it will be from dehydration or hypothermia. I didn't know what hypothermia was at the time, I just remember that the cold was becoming unbearable. From what I can remember I think it was about 24 hours we stayed in the back of the truck. Star and I huddled together to try and stay warm. Once he threw us in the back of the truck he only pulled over and came at us one more time. He said we were disgusting. We heard the truck pull over and come to a stop, this time instead of raping us he cut the tape that connected our hands to our feet, then he grabbed the tape that was wrapped around our head and face and pulled the tape off. I remember the sound of my hair being pulled out of my head like it was a loud drum or something. I had no energy left to scream or cry anymore, the only thing that kept me realizing that I was still alive was the constant flow of tears running down my face.

Get the fuck out of here, he said. Star and I looked at each other, get the fuck out now before I change my mind and kill you both. I remember suddenly having a burst of energy. We scrambled out of the back, once we were able to stand our legs gave out and we fell to the floor. He walked very casually to the front of his truck and started it up, before pulling away, he tossed the little black dog out the passenger side door. We sat on the side of the road in the dirt and watched the truck pull away. We were freezing, naked and in shock, left on the side of the road in the middle of fucking nowhere, but we were alive. Thank god ….. we were alive.

Chapter 9

WOW, I CANNOT BELIEVE I just put that down on paper. I am not quite sure how I feel. Anyway, what happens next in my life is something you think someone would dream about. You know when you have those strange dreams and you are not sure what they were about or why you dreamt them. This is one of those stories.

We had just climbed out of the back of the truck; we stood there naked and freezing. We watched the back of the truck drive away until it was completely out of sight. I don't remember the first thing Star and I said to each other, but I do remember I was laughing. Yes, I was laughing, what's kind of strange is that even today, if I ever talk about what happened to me to someone, I start laughing. Tears still fall and I start to shake but I will be laughing..(I know now that me laughing is a HUGE defense mechanism) anyway, I was saying please god don't let us have AIDS. AIDS was huge when this happened, it was a big epidemic and I was scared of it. I grabbed the little black dog and Star and I started walking. It was a dark twisty mountain road, with no sign of cars in any direction. Maybe he was hoping we would just die up here in the mountains so that he would not have to deal with our bodies. I am not sure how much time passed before a car came by. When we saw the headlights, our first instinct was to hide in the bushes because we were naked and bloody and I think stars nose was broken. We have to stop the car she said, we will freeze up here if we don't. so we held our hands out as the car approached. Of course, they stopped, it was two guys. Maybe in their late teens or early twenties. They got out of their car and asked us what happened. We told them we had just been set free by a kidnapper and rapist. I don't remember the look on their faces but I remember they were really quiet, oh my god one of them said. Get in and we will take you to the police. No, we don't want to go to the police. If we went to the police that meant that we would get sent back to juvy and most likely placed in another type of home. I think i have some clothes for you in the trunk I heard one of them say. He handed me a big long jacket. It was cold and stiff, but I couldent get it wrapped around me fast enough. Me and star and the dog climbed in the backseat. It was an older car,so it didn't have any heat. Where do you girls want to go? They asked us. Im not sure what we said but they took us to a park. It was dark and I felt really strange. We all got out of the car and sat on a cement picnic bench and smoked some cigarettes. Are you girls hungry, yes, we are actually starving. So we got back in the car and they drove through the Mc Donalds drive through. We sat in the car and ate and I shared some of my burger with the dog.. It was really quiet and awkward. They then asked us if we had anywhere to sleep and we said no. they told us that they could go get a motel but that we had to leave the dog in the park. I felt bad for doing this but for some reason I had no tears left in me to cry. So they went and got a motel. I remember walking in and feeling better instantly. I asked if I could shower first. When I walked in the bathroom, I saw my reflection in the mirror. I was hardly able to recognize myself. My lip was split in 3 different spots and my neck was dark blue with bruises. I stepped into the shower and started crying when the water touched my body where I was cut or bruised or bleeding. All the water going down the drain was red; I think that is when it all set in what had happened to me. Once I got out of the shower I saw that the two guys had gone to some type of store and bought us some sweat pants, T-shirts and some socks. The guys said that we could have the bed and that they would sleep on the floor. Once star was out of the shower, she put on the new clothes and climbed in bed next to me. They had decided that they were not going to stay the night there. They probably wanted to go home and tell someone about us. I vaguely remember them getting up and leaving. I don't remember what they said or why they left. Im sure they had to be pretty freaked out by the events that they stumbled into that night. Whoever you are, wherever you are in this world, I want to say thank you. Thank you for helping us that night, I hope that your memory of that night is not something that has haunted you over the years. Once they were gone, star and I decided that we could not stay the night in the motel because those young guys were probably going to tell their parents or call the police. So we left. We walked back to the park we were at earlier, I was instantly whistling for the dog, but he was gone, and I never saw him again. We started to get so cold that we huddled together inside the covered slide and attempted to sleep…..

Chapter 10

THE NEXT SEVERAL DAYS ARE kind of a blur to me. I remember sleeping in the same slide at the park every night. Star showed me how to dine and dash at a couple of local restaurants and I got pretty good at stealing from liquor stores. We still had the same clothes on that we got from the two guys who picked us up. Our bruises had turned from black and blue to green and yellow and the swelling on our faces went down almost completely, but we were far from feeling "normal". At the end of the 7th or 8th day, we realized that we were tired of living this way. We were tired, dirty, and hungry and we needed some medical care. We decided that we would turn ourselves in. I don't remember how we found a police station at all, but I do remember walking in the front door, and up to the counter where this woman was sitting behind a desk. May I help you? She said. I started to shake and feel nauseous and my legs got weak, almost to the point where I could not stand. I heard star say," we were both raped and we want to report it" I looked at Star and started laughing. The lady left for a moment and came back with three other police officers. They led us back into a room with a woman and a man and told us that we had to go to some other office to get medical attention. We got in the back of the police car and drove for about 15 minutes. Once we got to the hospital, we were led into the back area and they put star and I into separate rooms. They told me to get undressed and put on a gown that was open in the front. I had a woman doctor come in and ask me some questions, not about the rape but stuff like, does this hurt, does this itch, it's going to be ok blah blah blah. There was also a woman sitting in the corner of the room watching the entire examination and writing stuff down and making comments into a tape recorder. I remember them documenting everything. There was no blood, or semen or saliva left on me, I heard the lady say that into her recorder when they had the lights off and they were going over my body with some type of black light. The boot print on my neck was still bruised dark and it was obvious what it was from. They took many pictures of that. And when it came time for them to examine my vagina, that's when the tears started to fall. I had tears and bruising and the doctor said I had some splinters and foreign object matter imbedded in the skin of my labia. It seemed like the exam went on forever. All I could do was stare at the plain white ceiling above and feel reassured that I would be back with Star soon. It had only been around 12 days since we had met each other and planned our big escape from the foster home, but after what we went through I felt like she was my best friend in the whole world. After the physical exam was done, I put my clothes back on and was led into another room. There were two men in the room, one was sitting behind a desk and the other was in the corner with a tape recorder. I was asked questions for what seemed like hours. When it was finally over, they led me into the front room. I waited a few minutes and then they led Star out there too. We were given some cold sack lunches. It tasted so good, I remember thinking that it was the best ham sandwich I had ever tasted. Soon after we were done eating a woman pulled up out front and we were escorted out to her car. She explained to us that they were taking us to a center for abused and abandoned children until they could contact our parents. We sat quietly in the back seat admiring the scenery of the drive. We got off a freeway exit somewhere and drove around in the mountains for a while. The trees and landscaping was gorgeous just green trees and bird noises. This place was definitely not in the city.

Once we walked inside the place had a warm comforting feeling to it. There were children everywhere. The front room was huge and had all kinds of games and activities. There was lots of happy chatter. The age range there was from about three years to eighteen I think. I honestly do not know at all, I just remember seeing very young kids and ones that looked grown up already. After a brief tour of the place, they led us back to the room where we would be staying. They said that star had to sleep in a different section than me. Maybe because of our age differences, I instantly started to cry and rebel. Don't separate us, you cant separate us. We can never be separated from each other. Star held onto my hand tightly but she was not as concerned about the situation as I was. She looked at me and said, it ok, I am just right on the other side of the wall. We will see each other first thing in the morning. That calmed me down a little bit but I was still glaring at the lady like it was her fault.

We ended up having the first decent evening we have had in a while. We took hot showers and ate some good food. We talked to a lot of other children that were there .I remember there were these two brothers there, I can't remember what their names are but i remember feeling really bad for them . The oldest one was eight and the youngest one was around six, or something close. They were there because their mother had beaten them and then abandoned them somewhere. They asked me why I was there and I just told them that a bad guy got a hold of me for a while. I did not want to dampen their spirits by telling them my sad story. Their little hearts were already broken and I did not want to make them feel sad or scared or anything. I sat in the activity room with them and played around 40 game of connect four with them. I was giving them chancies most of the time; they were so excited that they were winning. When it was time for bed all the light went out in the front room and the staff walked around and made sure that everyone one was in their own beds.. It felt great to sleep in a bed even though the sheets had the same bleach smell that the bedding in juvy did. It didn't matter though. I was safe and I fell asleep tight away. When I woke up, I walked around to the other side of the hall and looked for start. I wanted her to go to breakfast with me. I didn't see her in her room so I went out to the front activity room to see if I could find her there. When I saw the staff woman walking around I stopped her and asked her where star was. The woman looked at me with sad eyes and told me that they contacted stars parents and drove her to the airport late last night and flew her back to Oregon. I started crying, and fell to my knees and started screaming. Like something you would see in a movie. I started cussing at the lady saying stuff like you fucking bitch I told you that you can never separate us. I told you not to, I told you not to, why why why. I started to freak out. I felt all alone; I went to my room and cried. When I was finally able to get a hold of myself I realized that I remembered what star had said her home address was during the police report. She said she lived on the corner of victor and B Street. I am not sure where this strength came from but right them I decided that I was going to somehow get to Oregon and find her.

CHAPTER 11

SINCE I WAS FREAKING OUT because star was gone, I don't remember if I grabbed anything from my room or the kitchen. I just remember walking out a side door and running for a while. Once I was far enough away from the building, I started walking. I didn't think that anyone was following me. It was not a locked facility so I figured they just called the cops on me. I was walking through thick bushes and I was scared, I kept hearing noises like someone or something was following me. I stopped walking and squatted down behind a tree. The noises were getting closer, and then I heard some voices. It was not voices of grownups though. I peeked my head out from around the tree and saw the two little boys from the facility, remember the bothers that I hung out with the night before. I jumped to my feet and walked towards them, WHAT ARE YOU GUY'S DOING? I asked them in a panic. They replied by saying that they wanted to go with me. I said no and that they were too young to be following me, and that they have to go back now. The youngest one started crying and the oldest one looked at me with a look on his face that seemed to be the worried look of a man far beyond his years. These kids have been through so much

I thought to myself. I didn't want to risk getting caught by taking them back and I didn't have it in me to run faster and leave them in the woods. Ok, I said you can come with me, but you have to do what I say ok. If anyone ever asks, just tell them that we are brothers and sisters ... let me do the talking ok. They instantly had relief on their faces. We walked hurriedly through the woods. I remember I was terrified of a wild animal jumping out of the bushes and eating us. I was trying really hard not to let the boys know how scared I was. They seemed to be kind of enjoying themselves by throwing small rocks and using their sticks as swords. I think I was enjoying the company.

After walking for what seemed like hours we came to a hill, we climbed up the hill and saw a freeway down at the bottom of it. Where were we, I thought to myself. Instead of walking down to the freeway I told the boys that we were going to follow it from up on the hill. I knew it would lead to some type of civilization, and I didn't want to risk getting caught by walking along the side of the freeway. I knew for sure that a passerby would call the cops on us. We followed the freeway until we reached a little city. We trekked down the hill until we got to the sidewalk and we were just walking looking around. I spotted a police car down the street so I told the boys to go to the left side of the street, there was an old shed there that we climbed into. It was a little shed with tools and weed eaters and shovels in it. It was cold and the cement floor was hard. We stayed in there for a long time, it was almost dark when we came out and the temperature was dropping like crazy. I was the only one with a jacket, but it didn't really do any good because it was a jean jacket, those are really meant just for looks.

We continued to walk around the city until we found a liquor store. I walked over to the phone booth and told the boys to stand right next to me while I was pretending to search for change in my pockets. Whenever I had the chance I would ask someone, excuse me I'm trying to call our mom to come pick us up, do you have a spare dime? (yes,phone calls were only a dime and cell phones were not invented yet) after doing that for a while I counted the change in my pockets and saw that I had enough to buy a couple packages of Twinkies and an abazaba. We ate the Twinkies, and were taking turns chewing on the abazaba while we walked around looking for a place to stay for the night. It was dark now and I knew that the cops would stop us if they saw three young kids walking alone at nighttime. I spotted a baseball field down the street and decided that we could go hang out in the dugout for a while. The temperature kept dropping and we were starting to shiver. I took my jean jacket off and wrapped it around the boys as much as I could. As the night grew colder, it started to become unbearable. We were huddling as close as we could but we were shivering so bad we could hardly talk. It was sometime in the early early morning, probably around 2 or 3am when I decided that we just couldn't take it anymore. We have to move boys, I put the jacket on the youngest one and told them to switch off wearing it every 15 minutes or so. I remember I could hardly feel my hands anymore. Let's cut across this field and see if there's an abandoned car or an old doghouse we could sleep in. As we were walking across the field I saw a police light shine towards the dugout we had just left from, run.... We have to run I said to them. We started running until we got to the end of the field but were fenced in. I scanned the bottom of the chain link fence and found a small opening. I bent down, and pulled it out towards me, quick.... go under it I said. The oldest one went first and then the younger one, when it was my turn I did not have anyone who could lift the bottom up for me. As I forced my body under the fence, I felt it cut through my back and tear my shirt almost completely off me. How strange that I remember the shirt. It was actually a pajama top. It went down past my waist and it had a painting of a rainbow and a toucan bird on it. Anyway, once we were on the other side I scanned our surroundings. There were no abandoned cars or doghouses that we could huddle in, but I did notice a park bathroom in the distance further out across the grass. We ran until we reached the bathroom. Once we walked inside, I told them not to turn the light on because we didn't want to draw attention to ourselves. We sat on the cold ground and caught our breath. It was probably about 2 or 3 hours before we were unbearably cold again. I turned the hot water on and kept my fingers crossed that the hot actually worked. It did. I let the water get warm and told the boys to stick their hands in it. We kept the hot water running with all of our hands in it until the sun started to come up. That hot water is what kept us from freezing that night and I was so grateful for it.

Once the sun was up, we walked outside with squinted eyes trying to adjust to the light. I remember the warm sun feeling wonderful on my cold frigid body. The three of us just stood there for a few minutes while I was trying to figure out what to do next. Let's go get some breakfast, What are we going to eat? one of them said, don't worry I will show you. Once we started walking, the younger one that was a little bit behind me started crying. What's the matter? What happened? Why are you crying? He told me he was sad about my back. Is it bad I asked him? He nodded his head yes. We walked back to the bathroom and flipped the light on. When I turned around to look at my back I was shocked at what I saw. Not only was my shirt ripped and hanging open in the back, but I had blood everywhere. I had dried blood all over my back and on the shirt. That fence cut me much worse than I had thought. I guess I didn't really feel it because my adrenaline was pumping and then, we were so cold that it kind of numbed it. I told the older one that I had to wear the jacket to cover up my back, and I grabbed the parts of the shirt that were hanging and tied them in a knot behind me as best I could. I bent down so I was face to face with the little one and said. Its ok, really I can't even feel it. I think I reassured him a little bit because he stopped crying and we walked outside again and headed towards the busy area of the city . We found a different liquor store and I stood by the phone again asking strangers for a dime. once I had enough I took the boys inside the store and let them grab what they wanted to eat. I don't remember what it was this time. After we had some food in our stomach, I told the boys that we had to hit the road. We walked back towards the highway hoping to hitch a ride from someone. I remember telling the boys, that if anyone asks, we are brothers and sisters and we are trying to get to Oregon to be with our mom. Let me do the talking I said. So we walked along the highway and I stuck my thumb out and waited for someone to pull over. The first person to pick us up was an older biker guy. He was big, with long hair and a beard and he had lots of turquoise jewelry on. He asked what we were doing hitch hiking, I told him the planned story. Not sure if he believed us or not and I don't remember how I found out which direction Oregon was in but he drove us in that direction for a little over an hour. Before he dropped us off, he gave me an orange and also handed me a big joint, be careful out there kids, theres lots of crazies and weirdo's out there. He wasn't telling me anything I didn't already know. I bet your wondering how I could hitch hike after what had just happened to me. Well I was thinking in my mind that the odds of something like that happening to me twice were pretty slim. Once we got out of the car, we walked in the direction of what looked like a big shopping mall or plaza. There were lights shining all over the buildings. We walked around until it was dark. I told them we couldn't go inside because we looked dirty and homeless and someone would for sure call the cops on us. I saw a couple of older kids hanging out in the back of the shopping center, they were practicing jumps on their skateboards, saying bad words and smoking cigarettes. I told the boys to stay where they were while I went over and talked to them. I struck up a conversation and asked them if anyone wanted to buy a joint from me, sure said one of them. He gave me 5 dollars for it. It was a lot for one joint but it was very little for three hungry mouths. I went back to where the boys were sitting and told them that we were going out to dinner. We walked around for a while and I spotted a Denny's down the street. Lets go eat boys. We walked inside and were seated by a skinny older woman with a raspy voice. You kids all alone she said? I am their older sister. My mom told me to take them out for a bite to eat while she shopped across the street at the mall. Don't worry I told her, she gave us money. I pulled out the 5 dollars and let her see a quick glimpse of it. So it looked like we had plenty. Ok she said what can I get you to drink. The boys ordered root beer floats and breakfast stuff. (even though it was nighttime) I don't remember what I ate. After we were done, I told the boys to do exactly what I tell them. Once the waitress was in the back kitchen, or out of sight at least, I told the boys to get up and follow me. Before I got up, I took the money I had and placed it on the table. I guess I was feeling guilty. We hurriedly walked to the front door. Once we were outside, I told them to run. We ran a couple of blocks, staying in alleys and behind buildings so we were not on the sidewalks where we could be seen. We came upon some type of car place. There were old abandoned cars everywhere. The chain link fence had a chain and a lock on it, but I assumed it was so that the cars could not be taken out because I was able to pull the fence open enough so that we could all go in quite easily. Once we were inside, we walked over to a really old truck. I think it was a classic that no one got around to ever fixing up. Anyway, we climbed inside and stayed there until it was dusk. I knew it was dusk because I couldent sleep. I put the boys on the floor and covered them with the jacket. I think they were able to sleep because their body heat was keeping them somewhat warm. I, on the other hand stayed awake freezing on the front seat, keeping lookout to make sure that no one was coming towards the truck. We left the out the same chain link fence and walked back out to a highway. We didn't get any breakfast this morning, we just went to the road and I stuck my thumb out, hoping for a ride. The first person to pick us up was a young guy who had heavy metal blaring. He didn't seem to care where we were going, or what our story was. He seemed like he was glad that he could help us out. We rode with him for about an hour, then he dropped us off right before he exited the highway. We continued to walk with my thumb out waiting for another ride. We were not that far away from our destination. I remember when we were riding with the old biker guy, he had looked up Harris and A street on a map and told us to keep on the same highway. The second person to pick us up that day was a fat man, probably in his early thirties. He had really thick black rimmed glasses and his car was a mess, mostly filled with candy wrappers and soda bottles. When I approached the car he asked us where we were going, I told him the story about how we were going to our moms house on the corner of Harris and A street, he agreed to let us get in. About ten, to fifteen minutes into the drive he pulled over to the side of the road and told me that if I wanted a ride the rest of the way I would have to let him see my breasts. I hesitantly agreed but told him that I did not want the boys to see what I was doing. I told the boys to get out of the car and wait by a tree until I motioned for them to come back in. I turned so my chest was facing him and my head was looking out the opposite window. I grabbed the bottom of my shirt and the underwire of my bra at the same time and lifted them up above my breasts. He was all fat and sweaty and he started making grunting noises, when I looked over at him I saw that his hand was down his pants and he was jacking off. I quickly turned my head back around so that I couldn't see his face. I stayed with my shirt pulled up, not only because we needed the ride, but because I was afraid at how mad he might get if I interrupted him. I tried to tell myself that it was no big deal, I felt like someone with no importance or value in life, so I figured what the hell. It seemed like it took him forever to finish, but once he was done I remember thinking how disgusting it was that he wiped his semen on the side of his seat, down towards the bottom. I pulled my shirt down and went to the side of the road to get the boys. I hardly said a word for a long time. We walked for hours and hours. Maybe I was scared to hitch hike again so soon. I knew that I should have just said no to him in the first place, but who really gave a shit anyway. Anyway, after walking for so long we reached a small community right off one of the exits of the highway. I was searching for a payphone so I could bum spare change again and get us something to eat. I stopped at a busy intersection and waited for the light to change so we could cross. When I looked up at the street sign I was shocked at what I read. I was on the corner of Harris and T Street. Oh my god, I said to the boys, we are almost there.. Ok boys, I said, all we have to do is walk for a little bit longer. Stars house is not far away, and once we get there, we can eat and take showers and sleep in a bed. We were so excited. I didn't realize how far away 'A street was. It was nighttime by the time we reached her address. As I saw the house that matched stars address, we walked hurriedly up to the front door and knocked several times. There was no answer. Then I rang the doorbell, still no answer. I walked around to the front window and saw a sign that said "for sale".. I stepped up into the bushes and peeked into a window. The house was empty. No one lived here. I walked around to the side of the house with the boys and laid on the grass and cried. What was I going to do now? We sat there in the grass for a long time. We were hungry and it was starting to get very very cold, I had to do something. We walked a couple of blocks and found a liquor store. The boys knew the routine, stand by the payphone and ask for change. As I stood there, I looked down at the boys, they were shivering. I could not let this continue anymore. After I had enough change to get a snack, I told the boys to stay by the phone and that I would be right back. I walked inside the store and told the employee that there were two young children in front of the store who appeared to be homeless or runaways and that he should call the police. I waited for him make the call. Ok I said, I will watch them until they get here to make sure they are ok. I walked back outside with tears in my eyes. I told the boys that the police were coming for them and that it was the best choice to make right now. The younger one started crying and I hugged him tightly. You are going to get to take a hot bath, and eat warm food and get a good night sleep somewhere safe. Are you coming with us? One of them said. No. It's not time for me to go yet. I will be ok. I need to stay here and find my friend, she is out here somewhere and she is probably looking for me too. You are wonderful boys and I'm so glad that we met. Please do the right thing, do it for me. Within a few minutes, I saw the police car pull into the parking lot. I told them that I loved them and that I didn't ever want them to forget it. I will never ever forget you, please remember that.. I stood up and ran to the other side of the parking lot and squatted down by a tree. I sat there and watched the police ask them some questions. Then I saw them both get in the police car and drive away. I sat there on the ground and cried, I cried uncontrollably for a very long time. I cried like I should of cried when the trucker let us escape with our lives. I did not cry after he let us go. Maybe a tear or two because of the pain, but I did not cry because of what the trucker did to me. I have not cried for it yet, even now twenty-five years later. I have always felt like what happened to me was a sad story I read somewhere and that those four days of torture in the truck did not happen to me.

Once I was done crying, I started to walk again. I didn't know where I was walking to and I didn't have anything planned. I kept thinking about the boys and I was shivering so bad that my teeth were making lots of noise by hitting together. I figured if I stayed moving that it would help to keep me from freezing. I stopped walking when I came across a building that read Humboldt highway patrol head quarters. I walked in and turned myself in. I rode in a police car to the local community police department. They checked me in and I took a hot shower, ate a cold sack lunch that tasted wonderful and got a cell of my own to sleep in. The scratchy dark grey blanket and sheets that smelled like heavy-duty disinfectant was comforting to me. I laid there and thought about the boys, I wondered if they were here in this same building with me. Don't ever forget me, because I know that I will never forget you.

CHAPTER 12

TWO DAYS HAD GONE BY before they came and got me out of my cell and told me that they had contacted my mother. They told me that a police officer is going to drive me to the airport where a steward will escort me on a flight back to LAX. I was just really quiet, I didn't want anyone to know that I was scared. I had never been on an airplane before. It was a small plane with only 15 to 20 people on it. They sat me in an aisle seat close to the front so the pretty flight attendant could keep an eye on me. There was a very large man sitting next to me, but he was nice and he made me feel better. The turbulence scared the crap out of me, I thought for sure that the plane was going down and we were all going to die. He reassured me that turbulence was normal and that smaller flights tend to be a little bumpier than the large ones. I could not stop eating the bags of peanuts they were offering me. When the plane finally landed I was so relieved, I took a deep breath, as if I had been holding it most of the flight. The flight attendant walked with me all the way down to the baggage claim area where I saw my mom and my grandpa waiting for me. I was surprised to see him there. He was not my real grandpa, and I never saw him that much, but he was the one who stood by my mom during all her childhood hardships. In situations like that, it doesn't matter if they are blood or not. Anyway, we drove home, I don't remember the drive or if there was any conversation on the way home, but I remember as soon as I got home I wanted to leave again. My mom had been notified about the kidnap and the rape but it was not mentioned. Maybe that is why it was weird for me. My sister knew about it too, but she never mentioned it either. I know now that I harbor resentment for the fact that they never tried to talk to me about it. Lets just ignore it and maybe it will go away. Life went on as if it never happened, for them it did anyway. I think I ran away again the next day. I felt like they didn't want me there. I felt like I was the bad one. The one who skipped school, got high, and caused problems. I just figured that my mom and sister would be happier without me there. I know now, that those feelings came from the low self worth my dad had instilled in me. He made me feel like I was worthless and nobody wanted me. I was also ashamed and embarrassed for what had happened to me, I thought I was doing my mom and sister a favor.

I don't remember if I mentioned this already or not but I was finger sucker. I wasn't the normal child who starts sucking their thumbs or fingers in the womb to self pacify, I started sucking my fingers from stress when I was around 2 years old. That is when my mom and dad were going through a nasty divorce. I don't remember it, but that's what my mom told me. In addition to sucking my fingers, I pulled my hair out. One hair at a time and twisted it around in a certain patter within my fingers. I pulled so much of my hair out that I had huge bald spots all over my head. I didn't ever try to hide my finger sucking. My fingers went in my mouth upside down, so it looked strange. People thought I was retarded or had a disease or something like that. Soon after running away from my mom's house I was arrested again and put back in juvenile hall. I was in there for a couple of months this time. I was having an extremely hard time in there. My hair was short like a boys and

I was sucking my fingers and pulling my hair out more than ever. The huge bald spots all over my head were great ammunition for being bullied and made fun of. I was also having a hard time at night when it was shower time. I was not used to people seeing me naked. I felt humiliated, like the whole world was laughing at me. All I would do all day is sit in the corner of the day room by myself and suck my fingers. I was so quiet that some of the girls in there thought that it was due to me being retarded, and I continued to let them think that to keep them away. My mom always came out to visit me and that was the only thing I had to look forward to, even though I felt ashamed and embarrassed when I was with her. Probably because she never brought up what had happened, It was like having an elephant in the room and no one acknowledging it. I figured that was ok though, because I had absolutely no intention of ever talking about what I was feeling to anyone. I had spent most of that year in and out of juvenile hall. I remember they had to place me on constant observation because I would constantly carve on myself. Since it is a jail for minors, we had to go to school there every day. In the classroom, I would steal staples. All I had to do was put one in my mouth and they would never find it during strip search. We had to be strip searched every day after coming back from the schoolrooms. After school, they would put me back in my cell and I would lie on my bed and carve things into my arms and legs. I would cut with the staples so deep that I had bloody scabs all over me. I guess they thought that I was a suicide threat, So they put me in the dorm with the other crazy kids so they could keep a constant eye on me. The carvings on my left arm were the worst. There were more scabs then skin left and they had to put me in the infirmary until I healed. At the time, I didn't really know why I was doing it. Maybe I thought it was cool, maybe I thought it would steer people away from me. I don't know what I was thinking, but know that I'm all grown up I look back and want to scream out loud to whoever will listen that I was a young girl crying out for fucking help and it never came.

As time went on I continued to runaway and get high whenever I had the chance. I would always get caught though and I continued to be placed in group homes and drug rehabs, so many in fact that I don't remember the names of them all. I ran away from them all the time, except for the stints in juvy,where I couldent runaway, but believe me I tried. When it is all added up in time I realized that between the ages of 11 up to age 17 I was only free for a year and four months all together.

I had learned all about boys and men when I was around thirteen. I was not afraid to have sex after the rape, I wasn't a virgin anymore so I figured I didn't have anything to worry about. I probably slept with 5 or 6 guys the year I was thirteen but I realized really quick that, once you give them sex, they no longer want anything to do with you. I guess I was cute and I always had people that wanted to sleep with me. I became a tease. I knew that if they thought there was a chance of me putting out for them that they would keep trying. I learned how to dress seductively, make eye contact, and flirt, whatever it took to make them want me. I loved it. I loved the way men looked at me, it made me feel wanted and wonderful, something I was not used to feeling. Even if I walked across the street and I got an insulting cat all or whistle, it made me feel wanted no matter how degrading it was. I didn't like sex anyway. I thought it was dumb and didn't see what the big deal was, I figured they might as well be sticking their dick in between my toes or my elbow or something. It didn't feel good at all for me. But then, I knew in the back of my mind that sex really was a huge fear of mine. I noticed that my emotions became completely shut off when having sex. No feelings involved at all, So I figured I wouldn't do it unless I had to.

When I was 15, I was placed into a home that I actually kind of liked. It was somewhat close to my house and that somehow made me feel better. I needed connections for when I got out didn't I? I was sentenced to only do 6 months there but I ended up staying a year and a half until right before I turned 17. They had this new program there called "the learning enhancement center. Since I was a ward of the court I really didn't have the option to say no to this program..They made me do all kinds of different things that were supposed to make me use the left side of my brain. They were kind of fun, I remember one of the exercises was that they would show me a picture of an animal, and I would have to stick my hand inside a bag you could not see into that was filled with cookie cutters and try to find the shape of the animal on the card. I advanced quickly and I completed all their so-called brain exercises and got a plaque with all the staffs' signatures on it. Come to find out, I was the first person to ever complete this program, which is now taught all over the United States.

The time came for me to be released from the David and Margaret home for girls. I packed up my few belongings, hopped in the car with my mom, and drove home. I remember sitting down for dinner with my mom and my sister that first night home. It was weird for me and I wanted to leave instantly. Once again, I felt unwanted I felt like the intruder was back. I know now, that I couldn't have been more wrong, but I was young and I had been damaged and the healing of this family was not going to happen over night. The abandonment of my father was what made me feel like unwanted trash and the rape just kind of confirmed it for me. I actually stayed at home for a little while this time. I started going to a regular public high school. I was absolutely not ready for that. I still sucked my fingers and pulled my hair out obsessively, I was having more and more panic attacks when I was supposed to be on my way to school and besides I had not been in a public school since I was twelve years old. The only schools I went to through the ages of 12-17 were mandatory schools I went to while I was serving time in the system. It was too much too fast and I slipped through the cracks really quick.. I found comfort and solace in the loser druggies that hung out behind the school. I got back into drugs within two or three weeks after being released. I was snorting and smoking meth, drinking alcohol, taking whatever pills I could get my hands on and smoking pot whenever it was available. I had my own ways of getting whatever I wanted. Later that same year, when I was 17 I started to steal and found myself sleeping with men for random reasons. Like, I needed a place to stay that night or maybe I needed money so I could buy some clothes from the thrift store, or maybe I had to make sure I had dope for the next few days, it didn't matter to me anymore, there was no emotion involved in it. I ended up getting pregnant. Once when I was 15, once when I was 17 and once again when I was 20. I had no qualms about having abortions. I was a teenager who was strung out on drugs and had no place to call home. I got more heavily involved into whatever type of mind-altering substance I could. If someone had pills, I would take them, I would do acid, mushrooms, alcohol, speed, pot, I even shot up a few needles full of southern comfort. During all these years I kept as far away from my mom and my sister as I could. I was mean to them when I was around. I don't know what my young mind was trying to accomplish by being mean, but I do know that being around them was always uncomfortable for me. Once again there was that goddamn elephant in the room. I was always thinking that they were picturing what happened to me in their heads and never saying anything. Never a hug or maybe an "I'm sorry that happened" not one fucking word was mentioned about it.

That same year when I was seventeen, I was at a friend's house getting high one day when the phone rang. It was a woman named Stephanie. She used to be our dad's old girlfriend. She was actually dating my dad while he was still married to my mom and she ended up getting pregnant, giving me a half sister named Laurel. She lives far away so I hardly ever get to see her.(If you ever read this sister, please know that I love you) Anyway, Stephanie went on to tell me that our dad is dying. She does not know what he is dying from, but he only has a little while to live. I didn't know what to think. I called my sister and mentioned taking the greyhound bus down to Albuquerque New Mexico to visit him before he dies. We had no contact with him for all these years and we had no idea where he had been living until now. Stephanie gave us a phone number to call so we could talk to him. I don't think i called that day, maybe the next. Maybe we needed time to process what was happening. I remember hearing him answer the phone. He sounded raspy and hoarse but I instantly recognized his voice. Hello dad, this is Danielle. I remember his words being somewhat inaudible. I could tell he was crying and that made it even harder to understand. He kept saying that he was sorry and that he was dying. I have no idea what else was said in that conversation. All I remember is him saying he was sorry and dying, I kept going over that in my head for years. Was he sorry that he was dying? Or was he apologizing to me? I guess I will never know. I handed the phone to my sister, I don't remember what she said to him at all, if she even said anything. As soon as I hung up, I started looking at bus fares and stuff like that. I was planning to make a trip to see him in a day or so. Tweaker's are huge procrastinators, and I was too busy sketching out on dumb shit to actually make the plans and buy the tickets. A week had gone by since the phone call. I had figured out what bus station to go to and how much it was going to cost. I remember feeling anxious, scared, excited, sad, and mad and all these emotions at the same time, about going to see him one last time. I desperately needed this so I could say my peace to him and tell him that I forgive him. I didn't want him to die with regret. Later that same afternoon the phone rang again. It was Stephanie, I am so sorry, but your father died early this morning..................... That is all I have to say about that, for now anyway

That same year I met a guy named Joseph and we started hanging out, he was about 10 years older than me. We hung out all the time and got high together. We were really great friends, even though I knew that he wanted to sleep with me really bad. I think we were such great friends because he wanted something from me and I wanted something from him. Did I mention that he was a drug dealer, and he made his own meth in random peoples garages. After being great friends for about 6 months, I knew it was time for me to give it up to him. I really didn't want to, he was overweight and had really poor hygiene. But I had to keep him close so I could stay high. So I ended up sleeping with him. That's ok though, I figured I got a good deal and it was worth it because after that, I had more dope than I could ever imagine . Because of the drugs he often had erectile dysfunction problems which worked in my favor. So I only had to put out for him maybe once or twice a week, but I was set. I had a roof over my head, so what if it was a different hotel almost every night, I had food to eat, and he bought me a car, and gave me hundreds of dollars to go spend whenever I wanted it. I compromised myself like this with him for seven years. I hardly ever went out to spend the money he gave me because I was afraid to go out in public. I was completely paranoid from the dope and I would often have panic attacks if I attempted to go somewhere, and I would end up never being able to get out of the car. I would sit in the car for hours sometimes, smoking my glass pipe waiting for my fear to end. I remained absolutely faithful to him though, I was too scared to do something with anyone else for fear of him finding out and then where would I be, who would take care of me? How would I get high? How was it possible to detest someone so much yet, compromise myself for him for so many years? I realize now, that that is just the same thing as prostitution. Fuck.... Who knows what would have become of me if I hadn't met him. I was aware that he totally slept around, I didn't care though,. I didn't feel worthy of anyone's love. Wow, writing that down on paper kind of makes me sick to my stomach. If there is ever the chance of him reading this book I do want to say thank you to him. Thank you for giving me so much and for taking care of me for so long. With all other things put aside, I'm grateful that I met you, and you really are a great person who deserves to be happy. I wish you the best in life. During this seven-year relationship, I managed to get myself arrested many times. Since I was an adult now I got to go to real jail. I hated it in there, I would always tell myself that if I ever had to go back I would kill myself. I meant it when I said it, but I never had the chance. After my fifth arrest for under the influence and possession of meth amphetamines, along with a violation of probation charge I was sentenced to serve 3 years. I ended up doing a year and 8 months in a women's jail in Los Angeles. I served my time and was released. My boyfriend came and picked me, up and we continued right where we left off, I think I was even snorting lines off a Cd cover in the car before we got to the hotel. Four more years went by, living the same scandalous, self-loathing lifestyle I had become accustomed to. I rarely saw my sister, and saw my mom even less. I thought about my mom a lot though, I didn't like to think what life was like for her having a daughter who is a drug addicts.

One day when I was twenty-four years old, I was waiting for Joseph to come home. It was not uncommon for him to stay out all night, especially if he was cooking a batch of meth. So I waited and waited, and waited some more. Finally after two days I get a phone call from a friend telling me that there was a raid at the house he was cooking at, and that he was in jail. The meth lab was also within a two-mile radius of a school so his charges were going to be doubled. I remember dropping to my knees and sobbing. What was I supposed to do now? I realized that there was no money in the drawer and I only had a little tiny bit of dope left. I didn't even have a dime to put in the payphone at the gas station to make a phone call. After four or five days went by I ran out of dope and I ran out of food. My gas tank was on empty and I was freaking out. After not having any dope for a day I couldent even drag myself out of bed to take a shower. All I wanted to do was eat and sleep, like I had not eaten or slept in years. I remembered there were a whole bunch on MRE's in the closet. Joseph had a friend in the ARMY who gave him to him as a joke. Telling him that he should see what it's like to have to eat those for months at a time. I remember something about him serving in desert storm. Anyway for the next 5 days I lived off of those MRE's. All I had to do was add water and it was a meal. On the 6th day I heard someone knocking on the door. I thought I was having some type of withdrawal dream or something. Anyway, it was a girlfriend of mine and her husband. I guess she had heard what happened with Joseph and she figured it out that I was stranded where we had been living. They got me some MC Donald's, and put some gas in my car and I followed them to their house. As soon as I was inside I went into the bathroom and got high off the pipe that she gave me.. Once I was high and actually able to function again I decided to go find an old friend named Robert. He is just another tweaker that used to buy dope from Joseph all the time. Once I figured out where he was staying, I went to him and told him everything that happened with Joseph. I started sleeping with him that same night. I realized that I was starting the same pattern over again. I was pretending to care, pretending that I enjoyed having sex with him, even pretending to be his girlfriend. This lasted for about a month. He did not make as much money selling dope as Joseph did so we were always hard up to get high. We moved around from house to house, always spending the night somewhere different. I didn't get to shower regularly so my hair was looking all greasy and my clothes were dirty and stained because I had no place to wash them. Robert soon started getting into stealing things, car radios, cars, anything that he thought was worth any money just so he could trade it for some dope. During this time in my life, there was constantly something in the back of my mind that was telling me that I needed to stop this before I ended up back in jail. I don't remember what brought this on but I told Robert to take me to my mom's house and drop me off there. I was able to take a shower and brush my teeth and wash my clothes. After that I slept, I think I slept for more than two whole days. When I woke up the first thing that I thought about was getting high. I remember I was dreading that I had to call Robert to come get me. I realized how sick and tired of this life I was. I remember sitting on my mom's bed with her. Barely able to keep my eyes open because I had no dope in my system, I told her that I needed to get high. I saw tears coming from her eyes, she took my hand in hers and said to me; Danielle, why don't you go to rehab.

Chapter 13

WHEN MY MOM HAD MENTIONED rehab, I found that I was not against it this time. She had asked me many times before and I would yell at her for even mentioning it..Something inside me told me that it was time to try to change my life. I agreed to go. She looked through the phone book and found a place that seemed good for me. It had good reviews and it was close to her house. We called and asked how the process of admitting yourself worked. They wrote my name down and told me to come in anytime I wanted as long as there was still an available bed. I figured I would go in a couple of days, even though my mom thought I should have gone right then. I know she was scared that if I went out, saw Robert, and got high again that I would lose my way and not go. I tried to reassure her that my mind was made up to go, I just needed a day or so to think. I called Robert to find out where he was. I went to him and got high right away. I was not even with him for 10 minutes before I was chopping up lines and taking hits from the glass pipe he had in his pocket.. I felt myself starting to come out of the zombie mode. A few days went by before I told Robert that I was going to go to rehab. I don't know if he believed me or not. Well, I think he believed me but he doubted it would work. I managed to get a good amount of speed and $1,500 from him before I went, to help pay for the treatment. I also got a whole bottle of Percocet from a friend. I remember I was thinking in my head that if I go to rehab for meth I could take the Percocet while I was in there so that I would be able to sleep through the whole detox part of it so that I would not gain weight. Gaining weight is inevitable when stopping meth and I was terrified of it. In my mind, my looks and my slender figure was the only good quality about me. What guy would want me if I got fat. I drove myself to the rehab center and parked in the parking lot in front of the building. I sat in my car for more than an hour, smoking as much speed as I could before I went to check myself in. Once I felt brave enough I walked in through the front door and said hello, my name is Danielle Jackson, and I am here to check myself in. They were very nice and they made me feel somewhat at ease with the whole situation. I sat down at the front desk and answered many questions. How long have you been using? Eleven years. Are you high right now? Yes. Do you have any drugs on you now? Yes. Why do you want to come to rehab? Because I do not want to live the way I am anymore. The tears were pouring down my cheeks. They took my vital signs, led me to my room, which I shared with another young woman. They searched my bags and me. I voluntarily surrendered my pipe and what little speed I had left. When they were searching through my purse, they found the prescription bottle of Percocet. Fuck, I thought to myself, how am I going to get through this rehab without those pills.

That is the addict in me talking. When I say it aloud, I realize how stupid it sounds. Anyway, they took the pills from me. I tried not to get to upset and I reminded myself why I was there. I can do this. I can do this. I can do this I had to keep telling myself. When nighttime came, the staff there took my vitals again and then gave me something to help me sleep. I slept for almost 24 hours before I woke up feeling famished. I walked out into the dining hall area and took as much food as I could. After I ate I went back to sleep.

It had been more than a week of me detoxing and they came in and made me take a shower. The water felt great but all I wanted to do was eat and sleep. That is what happens when you detox from meth. It is as if your body is trying to make up for all the years it was deprived of sleeping and eating. After the two weeks of detox was over the staff started to make me get up, stay awake, and interact with the people there. The girl that I was rooming with was coming down off heroine. She was a mess. I remember seeing people come down off of heroine when I was in jail. It was rough. They would cry because their bones hurt, they could not get warm and they were constantly throwing up. I had it easy compared to her. As the days passed, I became more and more social. I was somewhere that I finally felt I belonged. We would have to go to group every day. There were 68 people in there and we would all sit in a circle. They made us write these papers called "lifelines". We had to write about our bad life experiences. Starting as far back as we could remember. After your lifeline was done, you had to read it out loud to the whole group. It took me about 3 or 4 days to complete it. There were no computers there so it was written by hand. When it was my turn to read I remember feeling like I was going to throw up. As I started to read aloud, the counselor stopped me and told me to slow down and stop laughing. I tried my hardest to stop laughing as I read it but I found I couldn't. I was able to slow my reading down so that they could understand me but I was laughing uncontrollably. Before I could read more, the counselor told me to stand up and take some deep breaths. He made me continue to stand while he explained to the group that my uncontrollable laughing was a deep defense mechanism. Then he stood up, walked over to me, and looked me in the eyes and said to me, remind yourself, right now that there is absolutely nothing funny about this. That is when the tears started to fall. I stood there frozen. I didn't sit, I didn't read, I didn't laugh, I stood there and started to shake while the tears ran down my face. I asked him if I could go back to my room and maybe try to read it again tomorrow. He said no, Danielle, as much as this hurts right now is as much as it is going to hurt tomorrow and for the rest of your life unless you get it out. So, we will all wait until you are ready… I took a few deep breaths and wiped the tears and snot off my face and I started to read. I remember the first sentence saying, my name is Danielle and I am from West Covina California. I continued to read the whole thing. While there was no laughter there were tears and shaking, shaking so bad that I kept losing my place where I was reading. But I continued and read all about my life and what had happened to me and how my father did not want me and also about how much I hate myself for being too busy getting high that I missed that last final goodbye with my dad. I read about how I felt I had been given one last chance to see him and I blew it because I was smoking the pipe instead. I remember getting angry after I read it. I started cussing at the counselor asking him to show me what fucking good reading this out loud did. Then I sat down, and group was dismissed. The next day during group, everyone was talking about our emotions and feelings and how we develop these strange defense strategies. And how so many of them could relate to me because similar things had happened to them too. That day in group when I read my lifeline was the first and last time it was ever mentioned again. The remaining 2 months in rehab I started having nightmares again. I used to have them a lot when I was young; I think that's why I choose meth as my drug of choice, So that I didn't have to sleep. There were many nights while I was a ward of the court when I would try my hardest not to fall asleep. It was like reliving my real nightmare over and over again. When I was high, I rarely had them. Now after six weeks drug free, I found myself feeling like I was back on the side of the road where the trucker dropped us off. I became that little 12-year girl again. I have heard that when someone stops using drugs that they emotionally go back to where they were in life at the time they started. This was so true for me. The flashback nightmares were so bad that the staff often gave me something to help me sleep, and the woman who worked in the kitchen would often make me some hot tea to try to calm my nerves so I could sleep. I finally came to an understanding with myself that I would rather have nightmares for the rest of my life and live, then to go back to drugs and die. The therapy at the center continued on a daily basis. The staffs were always trying to get me to invite my family to a therapy session. My answer was always no. I knew in my head that I never wanted to talk to my mom or my sister about what happened. I suppose that I feel like if they wanted to try to talk to me about it they would have tried when it happened. And I never wanted to talk about my dad to them either because they made me feel stupid for loving him so much and I felt that made them angry.

Anyway, 3 months later, it was time for me to be released, I was happy and excited and scared shitless. I had talked with my mom about staying with her for a while; So I packed up my few belongings and went home with her. I started filling out job applications at places like star bucks and home depot. Of course, nobody was going to hire a 25-year-old recovering addict who never finished high school. I was starting to feel like it was hopeless. And I know my mom was afraid of me going back to my old ways since we lived so close to all my loser druggie friends. All I had to do was make a phone call if I wanted to get some dope and that didn't only scare her, it scared me too. I had this sense of confidence in myself that I would not go back to that lifestyle. It was not hard for me to say no after that. I had been in so many drug rehabs in the past and none of them worked. Probably because all of them were court ordered, and what I learned from that is that you cannot make someone get sober by making them go to a drug rehab and telling them to do all this mumbo jumbo 12 step crap. I know that it works for many people and that is great, but for me personally I think that a person needs to rehabilitate their broken heart, mind, and spirit if they want to stay sober. They need to put their emotions on display and actually feel them. I just felt like I had to say that, who knows maybe that one sentence will help some troubled young people out there realize what they need to do to change their lives.

Anyway, I had run into many dead ends and I was kind of getting discouraged. My hopes of getting a job and getting a little apartment of my own were disappearing. Then one day my mom said to me, Danielle why don't you try to join the military.

CHAPTER 14

THE MILITARY, THAT WOULD BE great but I will not be able to get in because of my criminal history but it was worth shot. I read all about the Marines and thought that they would be a little bit too physical for me. I do not think I had ever exercised in my life, unless I was in a place that made us. Anyway, I didn't want to join the Air Force because I was not too fond of airplanes. The Army didn't sound too appealing to me because all the pictures I saw were just people running around on the ground with guns. When I read about the US Navy, it sounded perfect for me. I would be able to live on a ship, and travel all over the world. I tried not to get too excited about it because they most likely were not going to let me join. So, my mom and I drove down to the nearest recruiters office. I had explained to them all about my drug history and my arrest record. I was already 25 years old and most people who join the military do it right out of high school. I didn't care though, that was not important to me. They told me that I had to have a high school diploma or pass the GED before I could join. If I passed the GED they could start the paperwork right away by sending my arrest record to someone really high in rank that made decisions on whether someone like me could join or not. I had made the choice right then that I wanted to get my high school diploma. It might take a while but that was something I realized was important to me. So I told the recruiter that I would come back as soon as I finished school. I left my name and my number and all that other stuff that they needed.

A couple of weeks went by and I received a phone call from the recruiter, he said that he went ahead and submitted my paperwork up through the chain of command, and that they would let me join under certain circumstances. These certain circumstances were that I had to sign a bunch of papers stating that I would have severe consequences if I were caught using drugs. I also had to be sworn in all by myself. Usually when people are sworn into the military it is done in large groups, where they all raise their hand and promise to defend and fight for our country. When it was my turn, they took me into a room with someone who was very high ranking. I don't remember what his rank was because I had no idea about the military ranks yet. Anyway, I was asked many questions about my drug use, and why do I think they should let me join and stuff like that. I was scared to death, my hands were profusely sweating, I was shaking and my voice was quivering. This is how I usually felt whenever I had to go to court for sentencing. So, after my meeting with him he made me raise my right hand and promise to protect and fight for my country no matter what. After that, the recruiter drove me back to the office and I signed about a thousand papers. I also signed papers stating that I was in what they call "the delayed entry program". All that meant was that the US Navy already owned me but I was not going to ship out to boot camp until I finished school.

I had enrolled myself in an adult school program that was specifically designed to help people get their high school diploma. I worked hard, and I studied a lot. School was always so hard for me, and I hated it so much. I always referred to myself as dumb and I was ok with it. Nevertheless, I was somehow going to make this work.

It took me eight months before I was finished. I had been staying with my mom the whole time. As soon as I got the papers I took them to my recruiter, he said that I was going to leave in two weeks to go to boot camp. OMGosh was I nervous. It was April when I left and the school graduation ceremony wasn't until June. That kind of bummed me out a little bit because I wanted to have that ceremony. I had never accomplished anything in my life before. But I had to deal with it, they said they would send my diploma and plaque to my mom's house in the mail. Wow, this whole thing seemed so unreal to me. It was hard to believe that I was really doing this… The day before I was supposed to leave the whole family got together to have a goodbye dinner for me. I remember that I told my stepdad that I wanted his BBQ chicken and for my mom to make her mashed potatoes and sautéed squash. The dinner went well, but I could not sleep at all that night because of my nerves. Even sitting here writing about it now, it still makes my hands sweat and shake just by remembering how nervous I was. The next morning my recruiter came, my step dad was proud, my mom was balling and I think my sister really couldn't believe it was happening. I gave everyone hugs grabbed my bags, and then got in the car and drove away.

Chapter 15

I WAS SO NERVOUS, I also couldn't believe that I was really doing this. My recruiter drove me to this place in Los Angeles where I was to be checked in. After what seemed like 12 hours, they called my name, along with many other females and directed us to go to a bus. The bus drove to the airport and the flight landed us in Chicago Illinois. I remember it was freezing when I walked off the plane. I was used to the warm Cali weather. They made us be quiet and stand in lots of lines for things. One line for your clothes, one line for your sea bag, one line to have them chop your hair off so it was level with the bottom of your ears. So many of the girls were totally balling and freaking out when they realized they had to cut their hair. There was nothing fancy about the style either. They got some big scissors and cut one line across. Did not really matter if it was straight or not. I thought I looked stupid, but I didn't really care that they cut it. A couple days into boot camp I was starting to cry. Part of their testing there to weed out the weak is sleep deprivation. I was literally falling asleep while I was standing up and I think it was effecting my emotions. I thrived on the structured environment though. I kept my mouth shut and did whatever they told me to. I actually surprised myself by finishing all the exercise tests in good time, being that I was one of the oldest females in our division it felt great to be able to win those young ones fresh out of high school. After a few days, I became familiar with the routine and what was expected of me. Exercising was becoming one of those things that I was starting to look forward to. I enjoyed the rush I got when I was pushed so hard that my legs and limbs felt like jello . So, eight weeks go by, I pass the final physical tests and the written ones and then the day came for graduation. I got to be in a graduation ceremony after all. I was crying happy tears for the first time in my life; however, I continued to doubt myself. I used to think stuff in my head like "I'm not strong or special, boot camp is just really easy" Even though I remember seeing people on the floor crying cuz they couldn't go on anymore. People begging to let them go home, I thought they were weak, because if I can do it, than anyone can right?

So, after boot camp was over we went into this big classroom and talked about places that were available for us to get stationed. I still remember my options. I could go to La maddalena Italy, Yokosuka Japan or stay local in San Diego. I picked Italy right away. Wow, I get to go to Italy and live there for 3 years. I was so excited, yet scared to death at the same time. I hated the flight, I think it took like 16 hours or something. And I was sitting next to a really old woman who didn't speak a word of English. She kept pointing to her feet, when I looked down, I realized that her feet and ankles were really swollen and she was asking me if she could put them on my lap. I have always been such a fucking softie that of course I said yes. So many people in my life have misjudged my big heart for someone who is being taken advantage of and it pisses me off. I know the difference, it made me happy to be able to help her and make her feel better.

Anyway, so I finally get to Italy. There was supposed to be someone waiting for me with a sign when I stepped off the airplane but no one was there. I found out later that the person waiting for me figured I was not on the plane because I didn't come out right away. I think I was the last person to get off the flight. I had to wait for the old woman to stand up so that I could get out. So it is almost nighttime and I'm in an airport in Italy. I see nothing around me in English, im starting to have a panic attack. I walk over to a restroom pulling all my luggage on one of those small metal things with wheels. I walk into a stall, take some deep breaths, and try to calm down. I am totally crying though. After a few minutes, I walk out and go to grab my luggage and notice that it is on the floor. Someone came in and stole my little wheel cart for my suitcases. I guess my adrenaline kicked in because I hauled the sea bag on my back and grabbed a suitcase in each hand. I started to ask around if anyone spoke English and I was not having any luck. A couple of hours went by before I found someone who spoke some English. All I had to tell him was NAVY. He led me over to the bus station and spoke with the ticket man for me. I handed him some of my Italian money that I took with me for the trip. So, he shows me where to wait for the bus. The bus ride was more than 2 hours and I was skeptical if I was headed in the right direction. I was crying the whole time on the bus and many of the passengers were staring at me. Once the bus ride was over, I saw that I was surrounded by water. I did the same routine, walked around until I found someone who could help. I bought a ferry ticket and followed people getting on it. The ferry ride was about 20 minutes. Once I got off, I started asking around again. I was coming up to people saying NAVY and putting my hands up as if to say where. Finally, this one older man offered to take one of my suitcases, he then walked me down the street for about 5 minutes and showed me an office door that said US NAVY. I thanked him and knocked on the door.

Someone in uniform answered the door. I was so relieved. I explained the situation to them in the office and they were shocked that I made it here all by myself. From there though, I had to take another ferry to get to the ship I was stationed on. When I finally got to the ship, I was showed to my rack. I leaned my bags up against the wall, climbed inside and slept. The following day people kept saying how impressed they were that I was able to make it to the island without an escort. I just figured they were saying that to make me feel good, anyone would of done the same thing right? The next week was all about I was adjusting to life on the ship, I found the experience to be awesome, interesting, confusing and somewhat scary at the same time, and wow, I gave myself a new life. I remember the first time my ship pulled out to go underway, I was so excited. I remember watching the routine as the mooring lines were being pulled. I still vividly remember the smell of the salt water, and the rust, and how I could feel the vibration of the propellers under my feet. I was what they called an MS. It means mess management specialist. In civilian terms, I was a cook. Being a cook on a navy ship is one of the hardest jobs there is when you are out to sea. We had to be in the galley by 4am to cook breakfast, and we were the last to finish up after the galley was cleaned from dinner. I loved being a cook, while most people bitched and complained about hard it was, I thrived. There was class on board the ship that they made the newest people take. It was all about common customs and courtesies to the local Italian people. There were many things that Americans do that were offensive to the Italians, and this class was to teach us the proper ways to act while out in town. When I went into the classroom and picked a seat in the back row, I caught a glimpse of a very good-looking guy up towards the front of the room. During the class, he had asked a couple of questions and that is when I realized that he was an MS also. After making a few friends I started to go out in town more often, it was so surreal to me that I was actually living in Italy. My friends and I would go shopping after work, and we were always trying new things to eat. I would always close my eyes and point to something on the menu, it was in Italian anyway so I could not read it. But, I loved the excitement of not knowing what was going to be brought out on my plate. We figured out where our favorite spots were, we had our usual steak house we ate at and for afterwards, we had our favorite bar where we would go and drink big beers. My friends and I started to form a little group of friends that were always together. We never went anywhere without each other. We all just clicked together and our friend ships were everlasting. It was a group a group of six of us, and in this group of friends was the real good-looking guy I spotted when I first got there. We were only friends though, at first anyway. It took me a long time before I slept with him. I knew that once we had sex our friendship would be over and I did not want that at all. When the day came for us to spend a night together, I was freaked out about where my emotions were and how I was feeling. I was actually enjoying having sex with him, this was an absolute first for me. After the deed was done, I automatically assumed he would not want anything more to do with me so I left. He had asked me to spend the night but I declined. The next day at work, he asked me if I was going to come back over again tonight. Sure, I said. But when it came time I didn't go. I was living a new life and I was not going to allow anyone to take advantage of me like that anymore. Anyway, to make a long story short, we fell head over heels, completely in love with each other. I had never felt happiness like that in my life. I also realized a lot about myself, I was so attentive and understanding and I opened up my whole heart to him. After his three years on the ship was over it was time for him to transfer. A couple of weeks before he was due to ship out he took me for a drive, so we could spend a romantic night together. Now this next part sounds like something out of a fairy tale. We drove to a different part of the island where we could visit the Castle Sardo. It was this amazing old castle, we walked up to the very top of it, I felt like I could see the whole world from up there. It was so beautiful. Then He got down on one knee and asked if I would be his forever. All the surrounding tourists were watching and clapping. I thought he was joking with me at first and could not believe that someone like him would want to marry someone like me. Then I saw the look in his eyes and when I realized he was for real, I said yes.

Chapter 16

WHEN THE DAY CAME FOR my future husband to leave, I was devastated. I had taken a couple of days leave from the ship just so I would have some time to cry and adjust to the fact that I had to continue these next nine months on the ship without him. Since we planned on getting married I decided that I was going to get honorably discharged from the US NAVY so I had to stay in Italy and finish up my four years. Less than a month after Randy left, I found out that I was pregnant. It was a good thing this time. I remember feeling that I had never been that happy before, it was hard for me to believe and I remember taking eleven or twelve pregnancy tests. I was taking birth control pills at the time, but there had been too many drunken nights where I forgot to take it. My usual day consisted of getting up at 3:30am going to work and meeting my friends at the local bar once we were off. We would sit and look out at the piazza and eat ciabatta sandwiches and drink big beers. Did I indulge too much? Yes, of course I did. Sometimes when I look back, I see that I just exchanged one addiction for the other. I was having fun though, and it was the most memorable four years of my life. When I realized that I was pregnant, it was so easy to quit smoking and drinking. There was a life inside me that I was responsible for, and I was going to make sure he/ she got the best of everything. Soon after my pregnancy was documented, they transferred me to Norfolk Virginia to finish the rest of my tour. When I was 5 months pregnant, I flew to San Diego to use up the sixty days of leave I had on the books. My fiancé was there waiting for me to get off the airplane. We had not seen each other for five months and I was somewhat nervous. My body was a lot different from the last time we were together. Two days after my arrival in San Diego, we were married. We got married at my mom's house the day after thanksgiving. It was perfect. I was never one for a big white dress, and flowers and a huge celebration. Shortly after we were married, he had to leave again and go back to his ship. I did not see him again until it was time for me to have the baby. We were having a boy and we couldn't have been happier. When he came to see me at my mom's house, I was almost forty-two weeks pregnant with a 10-pound baby inside. We were both so excited to meet our son. When our son was eight days old, my husband had to return to his ship. I managed to put our name on the military housing list for Hawaii, that is where his ship was stationed at the time. When our son was six weeks old, my mom and I flew to Hawaii. She was going to help me move in. For the first time in my life I had a home, I got to buy a bed and some couches. I hung pictures up on the walls. Life was great.

We both decided that we did not want to put our baby in day care at such a young age. I was breast-feeding and I wanted to be home. After my mom left things were somewhat tough. I realized I was on my own, in a new house, in a different part of the world with a new baby. The ship my husband was on at the time was a brand new NAVY ship and it was deployed six to nine months out of every year for the three years we were stationed there. When our son was eighteen months old, I realized I was pregnant again. I used to always joke to him about how lucky he was that he missed both of my pregnancies, I am extremely emotional and moody naturally. When

I was pregnant, it was twenty times worse. When I gave birth to our daughter, my husband was able to take two weeks leave from the ship. Since I had a c-section with our son, I was scheduled to have to have a c-section with my daughter too. The hospital where I had my daughter was a training hospital, and even though there was an experienced doctor in the room during the surgery, I was somehow sewed back together wrong. My incision burst open two days after the surgery. The whole in my abdomen was too large to cauterize and since the tissues on the inside had started to heal themselves, they could not stitch it closed. Nine days after my daughter was born my husband had to go back out to sea. It was a hard time for me. I had a two-year-old son, and a newborn daughter. The whole in my abdomen was healing from the inside out, and I had to stick my fingers into it and open it up many times a day and wash it clean to prevent infection. It was such a huge hole that I found it made me queasy to look at .I was told not to vacuum, or walk up the stairs or carry anything heavier than 10 pounds. There was no way that I could follow those rules. I had two small children to take care of without any help. I learned a lot about myself during that time. I was realizing that I was a strong woman and that I was doing things that many women could not do. when my daughter was eight months old our time in Hawaii was up. We picked military orders to go to Yokosuka Japan. My husband was gone for the pack out so I had to make sure everything was packed up and shipped to Japan so that it would be there waiting for us when we got there. The good thing about Japan is that my husband was on shore duty, which means that it is kind of like a 9-5 job. He does not have to go out to sea. I have to admit that it was an adjustment for me. Since he was gone so much in Hawaii, the kids did not really want a whole lot to do with him. He tried all the time but they would cry for me and he would get frustrated. Shortly after we arrived in Japan, I got a job on the Navy base working as the night manager for the officers club. I would leave at about five o'clock and come home around one or two AM. This really gave my husband the opportunity he needed to get to know the kids better. It was healthy for all four of us. I began to notice a new pattern emerging from me though. When I would get home, and everyone else was sleeping, I would drink. It was always a nighttime thing for me though. I would occasionally go out with some girlfriends I met on the base, but I preferred to drink at home alone. Getting drunk before I went to bed would reassure me that I would not have flashback nightmares. My husband knew that something bad had happened to me in my past, but I never told him what it was. I think that is maybe why he never pushed me too hard to slow down my drinking. He got onto me a few times about it, but I continued to drink.

It was in Japan when I started to write my life story. I had attempted to go to therapy and try to deal with my past, but I kept being turned away. I was always honest about my substance abuse, when the therapist would ask me how much I drank, I would tell him/her. Then he told me that I had to get a handle on my substance abuse problems before he could start my therapy. That seemed backwards to me, I Know that the reason I have substance issues is because of certain things that have happened to me in my life. If I am able to talk about the rape and the issues with my dad then maybe my heart would heal and I would not want to turn to drugs and alcohol. I know that my low self worth issues came from the way my father treated me, and I know that the rape is why I get panic attacks and suffer from major anxiety. And since I knew these things about myself I was willing to do whatever I had to, to get myself better. I was never in denial about who I was, or why I did the things I did.

Anyways, after our three years was up in Japan, we decided to go back to the United States. WE wanted to give our families a chance to get to know the kids. My husband had to go back to sea duty and his ship deployed shortly after he got orders. I had to pack up my two dogs and my two kids and move back to the United States. I was excited to go back, it had been ten years since I joined the NAVY and left. Once we got back to the United States, we bought a brand new home. It was like a dream come true. We bought the house when there was nothing there except for a dirt lot. I constantly emailed my husband pictures during the building process. After the house was finished and I signed all the papers and went through all the power of attorney stuff, the movers came and unloaded our furniture. I somehow managed to arrange the furniture in the whole house, paint the walls and decorate it before my husband came home. When he came home that first time, I was so excited to see his face. He was so proud of me, and what I had accomplished, and I was proud of myself.

Chapter 17

THE FIRST FEW MONTHS IN the new house were great, my son started a new school, my husband was home a lot more and we were all happy. I still had my nighttime rendezvous in the living room all by myself. I noticed that I was drinking more and more and I was self-medicating with over the counter drugs. This was nothing new; I had been doing this type of behavior ever since I stopped using methamphetamines. I guess I just switched one addiction for another. I started to document what I did every night. I thought that maybe if I saw it all written down on paper that it might make me think twice about how I was living my life. A few months after I started to document my nightly activities I decided to try to get some therapy again. Since we are a military family, we have one of the best insurance programs out there. So I called and scheduled appointments with five different psychiatrists. All these appointments led me to dead ends. They all five told me the same thing, that I needed to get a handle on my substance abuse before I could get therapy. I was beyond frustrated. I have always been one to tell people to "talk about their feelings" I think it is amazing what talking about your feeling can do for someone. I can tell my wonderful husband anything, and that is part of what makes our marriage so magical, but talking about things like what happened to me are not something I want to talk to my family about. I think therapists are needed for situations like mine. Anyway, I started to get completely pissed off about the therapy issue and that is when I decided to get serious about writing about my life. I was going to give myself my own therapy

I had started this book while we were still living in Japan, right after I was denied therapy the first time for my drinking. It was then that I realized I needed to handle things myself. I had only started on the first chapter when we were in Japan, and then I was too busy with the pack out and the move so I kind of pushed it off to the side. I thought that if I really did write my life story that maybe it would be like therapy for me. I knew that it would help me somehow. I was serious about writing down every mind or mood altering thing I indulged in at night. Going back and reading it was a big revelation for me. I knew how much I was drinking and self-medicating with other pills and cough medicines, but to actually see it written down on paper is different. I remember thinking "wow" why am I doing this? Is this how I want my children to grow up? This is what my kids are going to see all the time and think that this is the way you are supposed to live. NO, this is not what I want and only I have the power to change my own life.

CHAPTER 18

AT THE END OF CHAPTER 18, I made a statement about how only you have the power to change your own life. The past three years I have been proving that to myself. I constantly thought to myself, "Why did I continue to let addiction win" of course, it is understandable. It is a distraction and numbness from your feelings. What sucks is that so many people allow substance abuse to completely control their lives.

When I first stopped drinking and self-medicating on a daily basis, it was extremely hard for me. I started to have panic attacks a lot, and there was this constant fear of everything. I was afraid to drive on the freeway, I was afraid to let my kids play in the front yard. I would not let my kids climb the toys at the park. The nightmares came back with all their strength and realness. I found myself walking around my own home being afraid of things that I have never been afraid of before. I would be afraid that my dogs were going to attack me because they could smell my fear and anxiety, I knew deep down that all these things were due to my past trauma. I wanted to drink and take pills so bad. I knew that if I just had a few glasses of wine or maybe popped some sleeping pills that my fear would go away. But that's when I had to remind myself that it would only be temporary numbness, not a cure. Within a month of me stopping, I actually started to suck my fingers and pull my hair out again. I am 37 years old, why am I sucking my fingers. This really bothered me, yet it was also proof that substance abuse does not "fix" anything. So I decided that I would try to go back to a psychiatrist and try to figure these things out the right way. I realized that I was excited about the idea of being psychiatratly evaluated, but I was somewhat angry too. Well, maybe not angry but I had this feeling of walking into the doctors office that had slammed the door in my face previously and telling them " you told me to go fix my substance abuse problems before you could help me, I did that. What now" Doing this has made me feel like so proud of myself. I decided a long time ago that I am going to live and be happy, regardless of what has happened in my life. I do not need to tell myself everyday that I cannot drink because I have a disease. I can have a glass of wine with dinner, or go to the bar on a girl's night out if I want to. I am in control of myself and it feels great. I am finally starting to love myself. By writing this book about my life, I have realized that I am a very strong woman. I have accomplished so much in my life. And I want people to know that I'm just an average person who decided that I needed to heal myself in order for me to be truly happy and for me to be able to be the wife and mother that my husband and children deserve. If you are not happy, with whom you are than you are going to float through life missing so many wonderful feelings and experiences

Sometimes if I am having a hard time feeling good about myself, I write down some important accomplishments on paper. When I read some things I have done, it is more realistic to me.

I graduated boot camp
Served honorably in the US NAVY
Ran a marathon
Wrote a book
Conquered my addiction

Quit smoking cigarettes

Went to college to pursue my career as a radiologist

when I look at it on paper it seems like I am such an amazing woman, do I truly feel that I am amazing? No, will I ever? Probably not. I have learned to love myself over time though. I believe that what is instilled in a person as a child is what they are going to carry for the rest of their lives. And that's ok, what's not ok, is to let your skeletons in the closet continue to make your life miserable up through adult hood and for the rest of your life. I have learned that I have absolute control of how I want to live my life. I have also learned that although therapy is great, you can also heal yourself by opening up your heart, and being honest with the ones you love and sometimes that means being vulnerable. Over time I have learned how to be self confident, I can hold my head up high for what I have accomplished and I can stick up for myself, and for the ones I love. I have thought many times to myself that if I could go back in time and change something about my life what it would be. The life I have lived has made me the person that I am today, so for that, the only thing I would change is the fact that my sister felt that not only our father had abandoned her, but that I had also. And I would take back all the heart ache I gave to my mother.

I originally did not plan to have this book published. I was writing it as a form of therapy for myself. Nevertheless, since I have gone back and read it I have decided that I am going to try to publish it. If my story can help, even one person out there in this huge world then it is worth it to me. If you are one of those young people out there who feel like you are all alone and that there is nobody who understands you, I want you to know that you are NOT alone, and if I can do this, anyone can.

Edwards Brothers Malloy
Oxnard, CA USA
December 17, 2014